NEEDLEPOINT DESIGNS
for
CHAIR COVERS

Judith Gross

VNR VAN NOSTRAND REINHOLD COMPANY
New York   Cincinnati   Toronto   London   Melbourne

Printed in United States of America
Designed by Loudan Enterprises

Published in 1979 by Van Nostrand Reinhold Company
A division of Litton Educational Publishing, Inc.
135 West 50th Street, New York, NY 10020, U.S.A.

Van Nostrand Reinhold Limited
1410 Birchmount Road
Scarborough, Ontario M1P 2E7, Canada

Van Nostrand Reinhold Australia Pty. Ltd.
17 Queen Street
Mitcham, Victoria 3132, Australia

Van Nostrand Reinhold Company Limited
Molly Millars Lane
Wokingham, Berkshire, England

16 15 14 13 12 11 10 9 8 7 6 5 4 3 2 1

Library of Congress Cataloging in Publication Data

Gross, Judith.
    Needlepoint designs for chair covers.

    Includes index.
    1. Canvas embroidery—Patterns.   2.   Chairs.
I. Title.
TT778.C3G75   746.9′5   78-25761
ISBN 0-442-22882-1

NEEDLEPOINT DESIGNS
for
CHAIR COVERS

Judith Gross

VNR VAN NOSTRAND REINHOLD COMPANY
New York Cincinnati Toronto London Melbourne

Printed in United States of America
Designed by Loudan Enterprises

Published in 1979 by Van Nostrand Reinhold Company
A division of Litton Educational Publishing, Inc.
135 West 50th Street, New York, NY 10020, U.S.A.

Van Nostrand Reinhold Limited
1410 Birchmount Road
Scarborough, Ontario M1P 2E7, Canada

Van Nostrand Reinhold Australia Pty. Ltd.
17 Queen Street
Mitcham, Victoria 3132, Australia

Van Nostrand Reinhold Company Limited
Molly Millars Lane
Wokingham, Berkshire, England

16 15 14 13 12 11 10 9 8 7 6 5 4 3 2 1

Library of Congress Cataloging in Publication Data

Gross, Judith.
    Needlepoint designs for chair covers.

    Includes index.
    1.   Canvas embroidery—Patterns.   2.   Chairs.
I.   Title.
TT778.C3G75   746.9'5   78-25761
ISBN 0-442-22882-1

DEDICATION

My debt is a great one, especially to the people who liked my designs enough to want them in their homes and on their chairs. While they bought and needled and enjoyed the patterns, I've kept working and dreaming and designing. Their gift to me was far greater than the gift I shared with them.

I thank my children, Michael, Susan, and John; my bonus children, Martha, John, and Gail; and the next generation, Alex and Sarah. They have all smiled on my work and have been showered with needlework as a result—a ready market for experimentation. Thanks to my grandmother, mother, and aunts for giving me a shoe box full of scraps and a needle and thread for my first toy; to the late Gordon Martin, my design teacher and friend, who gave me four old chairs that belonged to his family in Missouri and who taught me that old things are as beautiful as new ones; to my father, who had an idea and a dream and never gave it up—and finally something came of it. I want him to know that I have tried to remember that lesson always. Thanks to Virginia Lefferdink for her continued faith in my ideas; to both the Embroiderers' Guild of America and the National Standards Council of American Embroiderers for all the input, exposure, and developing time they have given me; to Astra and all the people there who developed my film and printed my pictures; to Anita Morisette who typed the way you are supposed to type and was such a special help; to Fay Natonson who has been an extra pair of stitching hands; and for a delightful experience in working with a constructive editor, I thank Ms. Susan Rosenthal. Many thanks to all the needlepoint ladies whom I can't start naming because there would be no end and I might neglect one by mistake. To all I have taught, designed for, and interchanged ideas with, my special thanks and love.

While I did all the designs in the book, many others worked them. With each piece I have given credit to both the needlepointer and the owner. And I thank and love them all.

Above all, my thanks go to my husband, who sent me back to school at the Institute of Design, encouraged me and loved me, and helped me to keep working. He worked with me, refinishing chairs, stretching canvases, polishing my chairs and my ideas, focusing my thoughts, and teaching me that writing ideas is not that different from expressing ideas visually. My love and thanks always.

CONTENTS

INTRODUCTION

It all began with my love affair with old chairs. I wanted to try my hand at designing a fabric for a Victorian chair. The idea had been pulling and tugging at me for some time. Then in 1965 my husband and I moved to midtown Manhattan to live for a couple of years. There I saw many contemporary and antique mixtures working together with a flair, and I had an idea. Why not take an old chair and use the forms that were carved into the chair, or the arm cutouts, or the back forms, or the leg forms and build a very bold, colorful, and contemporary design that went with the chair? Behold! The chair would be neither old nor new, but a total artistic entity that was special, with its own identity. It would be like a piece of art—a useful, yet wonderful-to-look-at object and a smashing addition to any room.

When I had moved back to Chicago, a close friend gave me an old chair. It was a serendipity and needed lots of repair work. So, I happily set about making the design and having the chair repaired. This first attempt was so successful that I bought another old chair. Then a friend said, "I have a chair. It was Bob's grandmother's . . ." Now twelve years have hurried along, chair design after design, and I have worked with fresh enthusiasm to find something individual in each chair to give the total chair a special appeal.

In my work I have found that many chairs—American rocker, Thonet Bentwood, Victorian, English, Chippendale, Windsor, Shaker, Provincial—have similarities in their basic forms. Knobbed legs, spindles, curliques, as well as shell, rose, leaf, and grape carvings were used in many different chairs from many different origins. From some of these chairs, old patterns were adapted and used again to fit a chair whose acquaintance I had yet to make. One of the simple devices I used to make certain that a design was compatible with a chair was to use the carvings and forms in the chair's back as the basis for a design or in the design itself. Then I can always combine natural forms, such as flowers and leaves, with those shapes; I end up with an aesthetically pleasing and satisfying design. A name, initials, or other embellishments could be incorporated into the design.

Now, after all these years and many, many, many chairs recovered, I am hoping you will catch my fever and use one of the patterns in this book for a chair in your home. You will find photographs of old chairs, new chairs, leaf and floral patterns, and many colorful, bold, and humorous patterns from which to choose.

Perhaps a few philosophical and practical comments will make your chair-work even more pleasurable.

Strive for precision in your stitching; the canvas should be well covered and carefully stitched. The design can be freely done, but again, your work should be disciplined and precise. As far as the designs themselves are concerned, remember that they were created by human hands and hearts. They were not intended to look machine made. The goal is to create a total, appealing piece, not a counted, exact replica of a mechanical form that is not attuned with nature. My concept of design is one of fluid, natural forms, coming together in a dynamic relationship. Sometimes you will look at a photograph in this book and at its graph and say, "Hey, wait a minute. The graph and design aren't exactly the same." You'll be right. The graph was the design I gave my client. The photograph is what actually happened. The results were pleasing to both of us.

I tell you this so that you'll feel comfortable in using the designs from this book. If you make a variation from my design, and you like it, don't worry a moment. Do the work as you really like it or see it. Don't feel constricted or hemmed in. Let my graphs and charts be your guidelines, but when you consciously or subconsciously feel the urge to vary them, do so! You are the one who must be pleased by your work.

In this book you will see chairs and coverings which have become proud lifetime investments. Locating or inheriting a chair, modern or old, has its own rewards; and then come the hours of creative stitchery, bringing years of pleasure in seeing and using your own work. So, go ahead. I wish you happy times.

Judith Gross
Chicago, 1979

Part I

GETTING IT ALL TOGETHER

There are so many good books on the "how to" of needlework and I wanted to do a different kind of book—one that would minimize the mechanical aspects and emphasize the actual designs. For that reason I've provided only the most basic needlepoint directions, realizing that if you don't already know how to needlepoint you can easily find more detailed instructions elsewhere; instead, I've concentrated on presenting more of the chair designs themselves.

To make it easy to use this book, I've provided at least one black-and-white photograph for each design. Sometimes there are several presentations of each design and some are also reproduced on the color pages. In addition, there are visual helpers for each design. The Graph Outline shows the design in easy-to-copy graph form. To save you from a cluttered, confusing graph, filled with tiny numbers and complicated lines, I've provided a Color Graph Outline for each design. The Color Chart Outline matches the Graph Outline and provides a number for each of the colors used. Where needed, it will also have letters for stitches and arrows to designate direction for stitching. The Color Guide matches each number given in the Color Chart Outline to a color name and the Paternayan yarn color number. Of course, you should not feel that you must use Paternayan yarns just because I did. They are the yarns I use, however, and recommend to my students. Where needed, the Stitch Guide also lists each stitch letter from the Color Chart Outline, the stitch name, and the direction of the stitch.

A Simple Way to Start

Since I found painted canvases very hard on my eyes (and no doubt they are hard on your eyes too), I learned very early to work on a white canvas with outlines only. While some people complain that unpainted canvases end up showing through the stitches, I feel that with a chair one must be practical. The primary need is to cover the chair with a firm fabric that will wear well. Properly done needlework, laid well, will wear and wear into heirloom years. Paint on a canvas pattern can't compete with properly laid wool on canvas. Good wool will win every time because it is so much more durable. The object is to produce a piece of fabric with needlepoint. If the canvas shows through, the fabric will not wear well, whether it is painted or not.

Yet, working a graphed design is a lonesome task and one that requires solitary concentration. That's why I developed a simple method for translating some of my favorite patterns to canvas. First, allowing some time and concentration to do it properly, you will set the lines of the Graph Outline onto your canvas. This will be easier than it seems. You will be using #10 mono canvas, which has ten threads per inch, and the graph lines are also ten to the inch. You simply count out the threads and transfer the design to your canvas. Once that has been done you will be able to speed along with the needling by following the numbers on the Color Chart Outline and referring to the Color Guide and Stitch Guide. Often there will be more than one choice of color scheme.

Thoughts on Color

I love color and I am hoping to share with you some of the joy all colors bring to me. Bright colors look brighter with dirty shades of the same color. Here "dirty" means greyed or muddied. Artists grey down a color with a touch of the color's complement or a bit of black. The use of close shades of the same color will enrich your embroidery, just as an artist enriches a painting. I was trained as an artist and I see no reason why the objects we use every day shouldn't be as enriching to the eye as are paintings and sculpture. So I have applied my ideas of color in art to the color in my chairs, which I really think of as chair sculptures.

Calculating Your Yarn

For most purposes in this book, yarn amount requirements are calculated on the basis of one and one-half strands per square inch. Each strand is 28 inches long. With the basketweave stitch, approximately seventy stitches are covered with one full strand of Persian Paternayan yarn on ten-to-the-inch mono canvas; one and one-half strands cover a trifle more than 1 square inch. I use ten-to-the-inch mono canvas for chairs because it makes a sturdy covering, and I don't think a chair needs to be worked on canvas any smaller. Mono canvas wears very well; plus the designs are defined and striking in the ten-to-the-inch frame.

Measuring Your Chair

Measure your chair or take it to your upholsterer and have him cut a paper pattern for you to follow. Sometimes he will tell you how many inches to make for full measure horizontally and vertically. If you do it yourself, generously measure the width and the length of the area you need to cover with the needlepoint fabric. If you want your seat to be fuller than it is, add the number of inches of height up and down needed to achieve that added area. To the measurements you take add 1 inch of needlework all around for blocking and for the upholsterer to work with.

If you are doing the measuring yourself, Figure I-1 will help you. The vertical line from A to B represents the depth of the seat; C to D represents the horizontal front edge of the chair; E to F represents the rear horizontal edge; C to E and D to F, the sides, will be slanted. Even if there is an area to be cut out at the corners, you must work the whole fabric area and let the upholsterer cut out what is not needed. This may seem wasteful to you, but for a correct fit and a beautifully finished chair, it is a necessary evil. If you have any doubts about measuring, consult the person who will upholster your chair before your final planning is done.

For chairs with upholstered backs and arms, follow the same procedure for measuring (see Figure I-1). Be sure to make both a front and a rear side for the back as well as for any fabric covered sections of the arms.

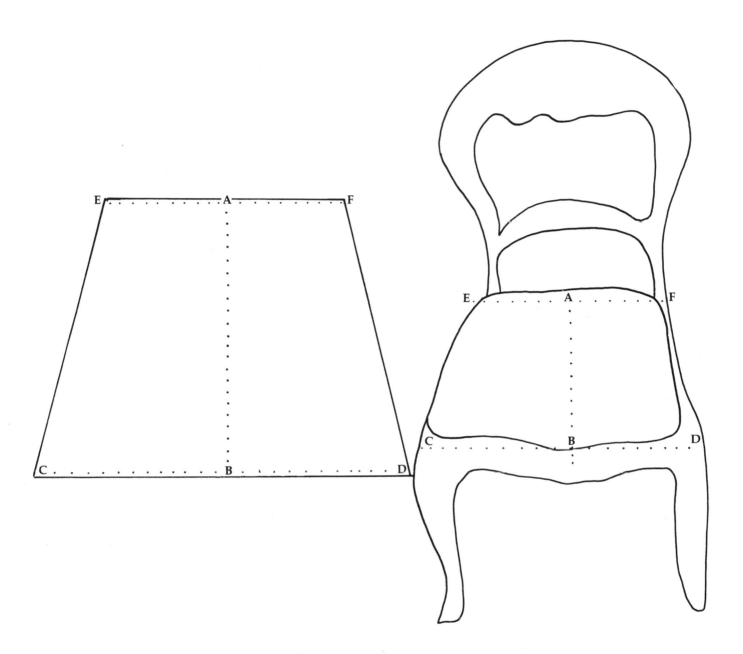

Figure I-1. Measuring your chair and fabric. Line A–B is the depth, C–D is the front edge, E–F is the back edge, and C–E and D–F are the slanted side edges.

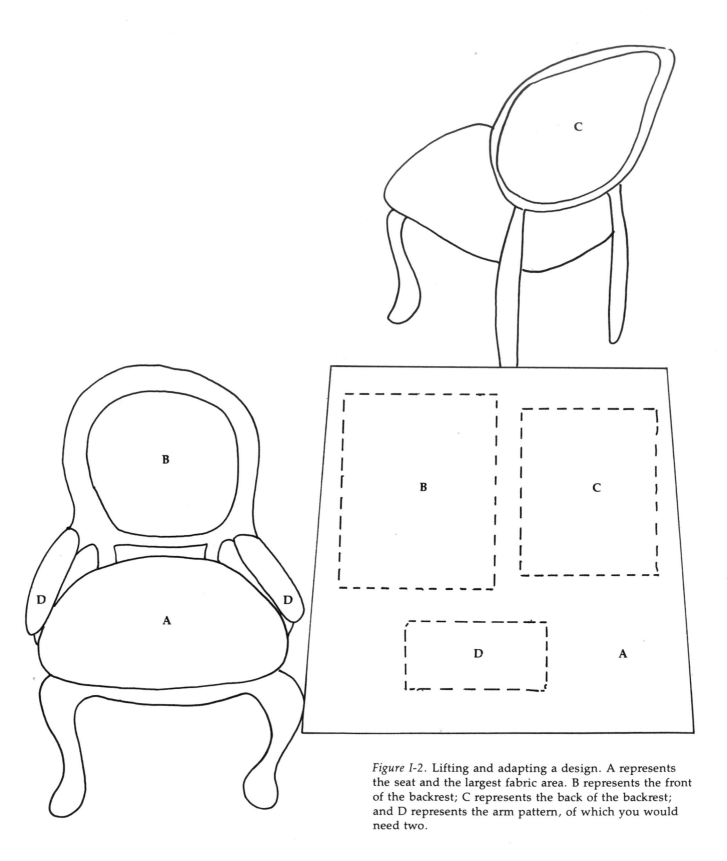

Figure I-2. Lifting and adapting a design. A represents the seat and the largest fabric area. B represents the front of the backrest; C represents the back of the backrest; and D represents the arm pattern, of which you would need two.

Transferring Your Pattern to Canvas

Each pattern in this book was done on graph paper with ten squares to the inch horizontally and vertically. In addition, every half-inch square is outlined with a heavier line. Midpoints of the top, bottom, and sides are marked on each pattern for easier reference. Use a ruler when you mark the borders of the working area of your canvas and mark the midpoints of your canvas at the top, bottom, and both sides. Be sure to leave enough blank border of canvas around the work for stretching and blocking; 2 inches all around is a good measure.

Draw your outline onto your canvas, following the graph and graph lines to correspond to the threads. Use a felt-tipped waterproof marking pen or paint your outline with acrylic paint, as I do. Once you have your outline on the canvas you are ready to take off with needle and yarn!

If, by the way, you are using acrylic paint, just mix the paint with water according to the directions on the container. Choose a thin watercolor brush with which to paint the lines of your pattern onto the canvas. A thin line is all you need. Wash your brush out in water when you finish and don't be afraid of the brush. You'll quickly learn to use it as artfully as a marker or a pencil. Let the canvas dry for a good 10 or 15 minutes before stitching.

Adapting Your Design for a Specific Shape

Some designs can be made to fit the required shape by merely taking the areas you need from the Graph Outline. Also, some designs are repeatable; you'll use the sections over and over again to fill the space.

For chairs that have backs and side arms, you can lift the sections you need from the largest part of the design. In Figure I-2, A is the seat and the largest part of the design. All the other parts of the chair are smaller than A. Measure your dimensions for all parts of your chair. Place the pattern for the B (front side of back) on any portion of A to make your piece. For your C piece (back side of back) use any portion of A. For D (chair arms) follow the same procedure.

The Basketweave is Basic

The basketweave (or diagonal tent stitch) is really the best stitch for a chair cover. Of the three tent stitches it makes the sturdiest fabric. The basketweave creates a double thickness by covering the underside, which increases its strength. Its interlocking qualities cause it to hold its shape. If you don't know how to do it, Figure I-3 will teach you.

The basketweave stitch is worked up and down along diagonal lines. You can start with

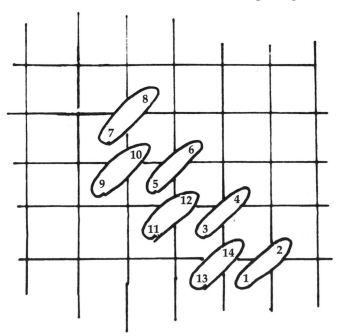

Figure I-3. The Basketweave Stitch. Bring the needle up through the odd numbers and down through the even numbers.

either an up or down row by bringing your needle up through the canvas at 1, down at 2, up again at 3. (Always go up on odd numbers and down on even numbers.) Pull your yarn through, keeping the tension even with each stitch. To achieve good canvas coverage and to keep your stitches flat, untwist your yarn while stitching. When you reach the end of the diagonal line, be sure to have your needle and yarn on the wrong side of the canvas. This is a handy way to avoid confusion when you are learning the stitch.

To visualize the space relationships for the basketweave stitch think of each thread intersection as a plus sign. See Figure I-4. Notice that you come up through the canvas in the lower lefthand corner of the plus sign (1), cross the plus sign and go down through the canvas in the upper righthand corner (2), and then you point your needle straight across the horizontal axis under two threads of the canvas and come out (3). Now that your needle is at this point (3), you are again in the lower lefthand corner of a new plus sign, ready to start another stitch. Continue in this manner for the length of the diagonal (4, 5, 6, 7, 8). This is in an ascending row. Now begin the next line in the opposite direction without turning the canvas around (9 and 10). When you are on the descending row (see Figure I-5) you cross the plus sign and point your needle straight down the vertical axis, under two threads of the canvas, and come out at an uneven number (11). Repeat these two rows.

While the basketweave is basic, you can use other stitches which are more decorative. Whichever you use, make certain that it creates a tight fabric. The loose decorative stitches have a tendency to pill, to loosen, and to wad up in use. Also, they make it easier for the wool in the yarn to catch on clothing, to tear, and to wear out more quickly than the tight stitches. With some designs in this book, I have supplied directions for stitches I recommend. Figures I-6 through I-12 explain how to do them. These stitches are often marked with a directional arrow on the Color Chart Outline. Turn your canvas and work your stitch in that direction. Be careful to keep your tension even so that you don't distort the work too much. Stitches worked at right angles to each other create a texture that is very pleasing.

In general, with regard to stitching, my students and I have found it helpful to work the small elements of color and design first. Then, when you do the larger elements around them, their effect becomes clear and meaningful to you.

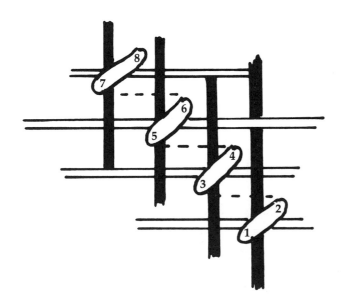

Figure I-4. Basketweave ascending row.

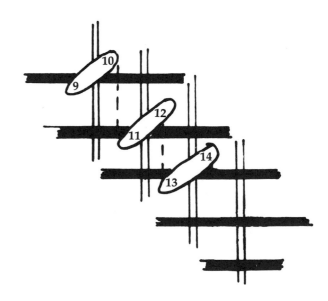

Figure I-5. Basketweave descending row.

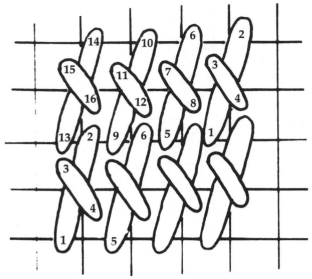

Figure I-6. The Knotted Stitch. Bring the needle up through the canvas hole at 1. Go up three horizontal bars, over one vertical bar, and go down through the canvas hole at 2. Make a center tie-down stitch (3–4) diagonally over the center bar and continue in this manner across the row. The next row is worked so that the top bar of the new row is worked into the last bar of the row above.

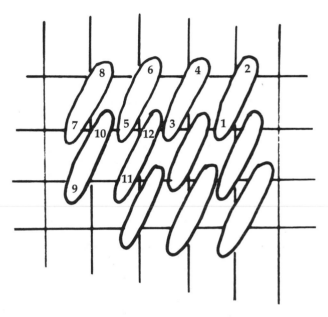

Figure I-8. The Interlocking Gobelin. Bring the needle up through the canvas hole at 1. Go up two horizontal bars, over one vertical bar, and go down through the canvas hole at 2. The next row is done so that the top bar of the new row is worked into the last bar of the row above. Rows 1 and 2 are worked differently (row 1 is worked right to left and row 2 is worked left to right) and are repeated every other row to continue the stitch.

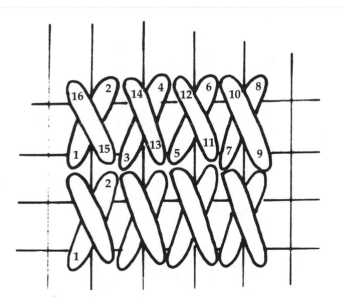

Figure I-7. The Oblong Cross. Bring the needle up through the canvas hole at 1. Go up two horizontal bars, over one vertical bar, and come down through the canvas hole at 2. Work from left to right across the whole area to be covered (1–7) and then come back on the same stitches, repeating the first row in reverse (9–16). Simply go up two horizontal bars and over one vertical bar, working from right to left to cover each previously made stitch. This is the same way the cross-stitch is done in embroidery. It makes a beautiful trapuntolike area.

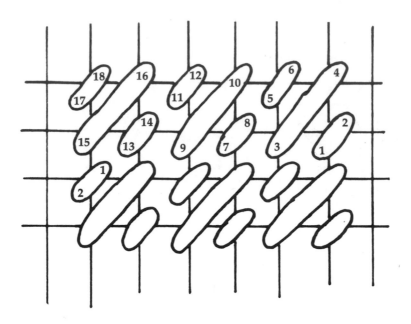

Figure I-9. The Mosaic Stitch. Bring the needle up through the canvas hole at 1. Over one, over two, over one is the chant. The mosaic stitch crosses one "plus" sign, then two "plus" signs, and then one again. The mosaic stitch is basically three stitches formed in a square box.

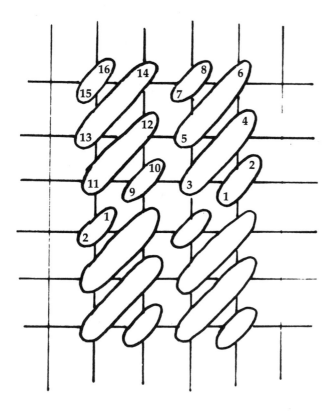

Figure I-10. The Cashmere Stitch. This is an extension of the mosaic—one plus sign, two double plus signs, and another single plus sign. The stitches form a rectangle instead of a square.

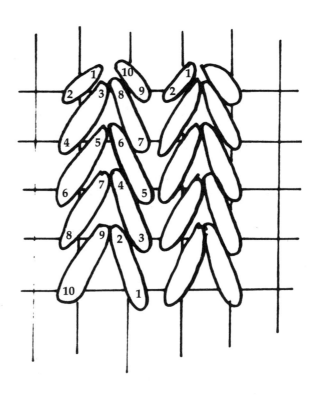

Figure I-11. The Kalem Stitch. The kalem and knitting stitches are actually the same stitch. The kalem is done vertically on the canvas and the knitting stitch is done horizontally. Bring the needle up through the canvas hole at odd numbers and down at evens.

Making Circles Look Round

At some stage all needlepointers ask, "How can I make my circles look more round?" Since many of the designs in this book incorporate circular shapes, it is important that you learn how to do them. But remember that needlepoint is built on a square grid, and so, no forms can be absolutely round. Your aim is to create an illusion of roundness. If the circles are counted out evenly, you will create a series of tiny hexagons or octagons and they will not look circular. Instead, they will seem stilted and boxy because of the static, counted way in which they were made. Don't be trapped by mechanical draftsmanship. The best way to convey naturalness and to achieve visual perfection is through irregularity and unevenness. The artist's device for creating this feeling of roundness is to break down the arcs and circles with small uneven irregularities. In stitchery, the visual illusion comes from the same device, and the best way to perfect this skill is to simply do it.

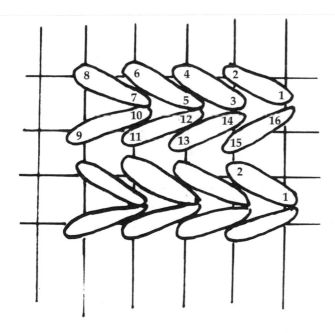

Figure I-12. The Knitting Stitch. This is the horizontal version of the kalem stitch. Again, bring the needle up through the canvas at odd numbers and down at even numbers.

Part II

CONTEMPORARY DESIGNS FROM ANTIQUE CHAIRS

Antique chairs from many periods were rich in imaginative carvings and shapes. They were created and built when carvings and wood sculpture made a piece of furniture more valuable; the more, the better. It was the opposite of the modern design philosophy which says "less is more." For my fabric design purposes these chairs provide a wonderful assortment of intriguing elements that I incorporate into the designs. Although the designs in this section were done for antique chairs, they add a warming lift to our more contemporary furniture, as well. As you will see from some of the designs in this section, I have particularly enjoyed the old Victorian forms. They are both nostalgic and humorous. On a Victorian or other chair they are perfect, and used on a contemporary or modern chair they are always refreshing and occasionally even startling.

Victorian Curliques

Seat Design (Shown on a Bentwood Chair)

Consider yourself quite fortunate if you are the owner of an old Vienna chair or a real Thonet Bentwood.

Michael Thonet was a young cabinetmaker in a small German town on the Rhine in the early 1830s. He was far ahead of his time. With the cheap and readily available red beech of eastern Europe, he produced chairs of bent wood, using laminated wooden strips. In 1842 at the Industrial Fair in Mainz, the Austrian chancellor, Clemens Metternich, asked Thonet to come to Vienna to make chairs for the Palais Liechtenstein. The chairs he produced for the Austrian royalty were beautiful and delicate.

Figure II-1. Bentwood chair with *Victorian Curliques* design. Worked by Judith Gross. Chair owned by Susan Gross.

Figure II-2. Detailed view of *Victorian Curliques* design. The seat is approximately 16½ inches (41.9 cm) in diameter.

(text continued on page 22)

Figure II-3. Color Chart Outline.

Color Guide

Number	Color Name	Paternayan Color
1	navy blue	#311
2	purple	#612
3	magenta	#644
4	tile	#234
5	khaki	#521
6	medium light magenta	#649
7	orange	#444
8	light orange	#464
9	pink	#281
10	light blue	#382
11	light khaki	#541

Figure II-4. Graph Outline.

In the late 1850s Thonet began to manufacture a Thonet chair for his own firm. It's twisted laminations exemplified fine craftsmanship with beautiful classic forms; yet could be mass-produced and would still appeal to the general public and to artists and craftsmen of generations to come. All this happened fifty years before the Bauhaus advanced the idea that normal everyday products could have beautiful design.

The most successful Thonet chair was copied in this country and became known as the Vienna chair. Companies such as the Sheboygan Chair Company in Sheboygan, Wisconsin produced many of these Vienna chairs. The Vienna chair we have today, with its 16- to 17-inch circular seat, has almost the same dimensions as did Thonet's most successful 1859 model. Remarkably, this form has been able to bridge the gap between the tastes of the eighteenth and twentieth centuries.

The Vienna chair is still being manufactured, bought, and used today. Its lines are free, circular, and appealing, and it makes a comfortable seat. It is not heavy looking and doesn't add too much weight to a room.

For an old Vienna chair or a new one this is a fine, bold, colorful, and gay pattern. I used a curlique form from another Vienna chair as part of the background structure of this design and then I built upon the design with more Victorian forms. The curliques hold the design together. The glorious, loud, contemporary use of color makes a delightful mix with the Victorian pattern. The outer ring of color was added to the Color Chart and Graph Outlines so that you could use this pattern on a larger chair. You can make the pattern as large as necessary simply by enlarging this outside ring. It can be adapted for a square or rectangular chair, too, by setting the patterned part where you want it on the chair (see Figure I-2).

Amoebas and Molecules

Seat and Back Design (Shown on a Victorian Side Chair)

This side chair is most likely a version of a French antique that was very much in vogue from the 1850s to the 1890s. The arabesque form is repeated in the design carved into the wood. I incorporated this one simple form into the design, but also wanted some organic forms to further develop the one shape. I decided upon the amoeba and molecule forms I found in my youngest son's biology book. They proved to be a perfect complement to the arabesque.

Figure II-5. Victorian side chair with *Amoebas and Molecules* design. Worked and owned by Judith Gross.

Figure II-6. Detailed view of *Amoebas and Molecules* design. The seat is approximately 26 inches (66 cm) in diameter.

Figure II-7. Color Chart Outline.

Color Guide

Number	Color Name	Paternayan Color
1	greyed pink	#281
2	bright red	#202
3	medium red	#850
4	dark gold	#427
5	medium gold	#440
6	yellow	#441
7	light yellow	#442
8	light greyed yellow	#015

Figure II-8. Graph Outline.

Autumn Colors

Seat Design (Shown on a Victorian Side Chair)

It was a glorious Fall and the leaves outside were red and golden with some leaves still bright green. So I took a handful of yarns outside and matched them to the leaves on the trees and bushes. When I had found some exact and lovely color matches, I chose freely from those I liked the best and put them together.

The engraved forms on the chair were used to achieve a tracery and light, airy feeling. Combining the chair forms and the Fall's gorgeous chroma, it was as if I were sketching my feelings about the chair and the Fall.

This Victorian side chair, with an open back and a single cross piece, was influenced by the Queen Anne period. When I first obtained the chair it needed lots of structural repairs. A skillful cabinetmaker got it ready for the stripping, sanding, polishing, and loving care my husband provides so well.

Figure II-9. Victorian side chair with *Autumn Colors* design. Worked and owned by Judith Gross.

Figure II-10. Detailed view of *Autumn Colors* design. The seat is 22 inches long and 25 inches wide (55.9 cm by 63.5 cm).

Figure II-11. Color Chart Outline. (A number imposed directly on a line indicates that the line is to be done in that color.)

Color Guide

Number	Color Name	Paternayan Color
1	bright red	#242
2	dark red	#203
3	medium dark red	#240
4	dark yellow green	#540
5	light yellow green	#553
6	dark yellow	#440
7	light yellow	#442

Figure II-12. Graph Outline.

Victorian Roses and Leaves

Seat Design (Shown on Two Fancy Victorian Side Chairs)

Figures II-13 and II-14 show two chairs that are similar but not exactly the same. They both have the familiar, delicate rose-and-leaf carvings; the design created from the carvings works well on both chairs. It would be appropriate for all of the small chairs of this type.

Some time ago, a close friend stopped by at her neighbor's. She was saying that she wished she could find some old chairs. Her neighbor asked, "Remember when we moved in I borrowed a chair from your basement to sit on until the moving van arrived? I am still using it." The chair

Figure II-13. Fancy Victorian side chair with *Victorian Roses and Leaves* design in light background color. Worked by Judith Gross. Chair owned by Carol Solomon.

Figure II-14. Fancy Victorian side chair with *Victorian Roses and Leaves* design worked in dark background color. Worked and owned by Judith Gross.

shown in Figure II-13 was returned to my friend, my husband refinished it, and I designed the chair cover. It now lives happily ever after in a thirty-fifth floor apartment, a Victorian gem made even more interesting by the modern furniture and art around it.

The second chair (shown in Figure II-14) is my own—the gift of a young man who was studying at Yale Medical School at the time. He knew what I liked, and when he found this chair he rehabilitated it and brought it to me.

The design worked splendidly for each of the chairs with only one color change made to accommodate the different color schemes.

Figure II-15. Detailed view of *Victorian Roses and Leaves* design done in light background color. The size is 18½ inches long and 18 inches wide (47 cm by 45.7 cm).

Figure II-16. Color Chart Outline.

Light Background Color Guide

Number	Color Name	Paternayan Color
1	medium brown	#521
2	brown	#511
3	canary yellow	#450
4	medium light brown	#445
5	light brown	#453
6	dark green	#540
7	medium yellow green	#545
8	beige	#455

Dark Background Color Guide

Number	Color Name	Paternayan Color
1	medium dark khaki	#443
2	medium light khaki	#445
3	navy blue	#311
4	medium dark blue	#381
5	medium blue	#380
6	gold	#440
7	beige	#455
8	dark gold	#427

Figure II-17. Graph Outline.

C-1

C-2

C-3

C-4

C-5

C-7

C-8

C-6

C-9

C-10

C-11

Color Plate 1. A detailed view of the *Victorian Curliques* design, also shown on page 19. Worked by Judith Gross. Bentwood chair owned by Susan Gross.

Color Plate 2. The *Amoebas and Molecules* design was made for the seat and back of a Victorian side chair. See page 22. Worked and owned by Judith Gross.

Color Plate 3. The seat of this fancy Victorian side chair was covered with the *Victorian Roses and Leaves* design. The design can also be done in an alternate color scheme for drastically different results. See page 29. Worked by Judith Gross. Chair owned by Carol Solomon.

Color Plate 4. The *Floral Arabesque* design was done for the seat of a kitchen/opera chair. See page 40. Worked and owned by Susan Gross.

Color Plate 5. Detailed view of the top of an American rocker that was covered with the *Roses and Swirls* design. See page 52. Worked by Bunny Factor. Chair owned by Pat Cohen.

Color Plate 6. Detail of the seat of a fancy rocker worked in the *Swirling Leaves* design, also shown on page 59. Worked and owned by Jean Goldberg.

Color Plate 7. A detailed view of the *Circles in Motion* design done for a traditional Windsor chair. See page 63. Worked by Janis Bente. Owned by Mr. and Mrs. James Bente.

Color Plate 8. A detailed view of the *Manhole Covers* design done for a contemporary Windsor chair pad. See page 103. Worked and owned by Carol Solomon.

Color Plate 9. The *Elm, Maple, and Locust Leaves* design, also shown on page 68. Worked and owned by Mrs. Robert M. Eckhouse.

Color Plate 10. A detailed view of the *Split-Leaf Philodendra* design. See page 72. Worked and owned by Gail Harnett.

Color Plate 11. The *Snowflakes* design done on a heart-shaped-back chair. The same design done on a Bentwood chair and a piano bench can be seen on page 84. Worked by Judith Gross. Chair owned by Mr. and Mrs. Morton J. Harris.

C-12

C-13

C-15

C-14

C-16

Color Plate 12. The *Formal Leaves* design, also shown on page 91. Worked by Kay Frank. Chippendale chair owned by Dr. and Mrs. Richard Burnstine.

Color Plate 13. A detailed view of the *Grapes and Leaves* design. See page 99. Worked and owned by Mrs. Robert M. Eckhouse.

Color Plate 14. *Name and Birthdate* design done on a child's chair. See page 109. Worked by Judith Gross. Chair owned by Alex Gross.

Color Plate 15. *Spring Daisies* design done for a footstool, also shown on page 115. Worked and owned by Mrs. Edward G. Bazelon.

Color Plate 16. The *Chair and Plants Collage* chair-pad design worked on a Bertoia/Knoll chair. See page 121. This chair pad is part of a set of six. Each pad has similar coloring, but no two pads are exactly alike. Worked and owned by Judith Gross.

Color Plate 17. Another of the set of six chair pads for the Bertoia/Knoll chair shown in Color Plate 16. Worked and owned by Judith Gross.

C-17

Danish and Bold

Seat Design (Shown on a High-Back Piano Stool)

Some friends of mine, who were at a party given in an old house in Hammond, Indiana, were told by their host that he was about to give away three old matching chairs that were in the attic. Since each of the three visiting couples wanted them, the host had to play King Solomon and give one to each couple.

This Victorian chair is an adjustable piano chair with glass-ball claw feet and is quite rare. The contemporary pattern was developed from the forms in the chair and its rungs were abstracted and made gently humorous. I used bold Danish colors, which harmonize with the owners' striking Danish modern furniture. The chair is no longer either old or new. Chair and cover combine to make a sculpture to sit upon; a total whole; a visual delight, as well as a utilitarian seat.

Figure II-18. High-back piano stool with *Danish and Bold* design. Worked and owned by Patricia Blank.

Figure II-19. Detailed view of *Danish and Bold* design. The size is 18 inches (45.7 cm) in diameter.

Figure II-20. Color Chart Outline.

Color Guide

Number	Color Name	Paternayan Color
1	bright orange	#434
2	dark navy blue	#311
3	yellow	#441
4	dark khaki	#521
5	medium blue	#381
6	dark green	#540
7	dark yellow	#447

Figure II-21. Graph Outline.

Morning Glories and Swirls

Seat Design (Shown on a Kitchen/Opera Chair)

During the nineteenth century, the common, practical wooden chair brought from Europe by early urban settlers seemed to reach every part of North America. It was often made locally in the available wood—oak, hickory, maple, pine—depending upon the chair maker's supply and the market's demands. And, depending upon the use, the chair had cane seats, was padded, or had hard wooden seats. Sometimes the seat was shaped to fit the body; most often it was not.

The most fascinating features of this chair are the carving in the top rail of the back and the occasional rungs or spindles which were either hand-cut or machine-turned. The carving was often done by hand, free style, or was done from a template by hand or with a wood lathe.

The chairs were used everywhere—in the big farm kitchens, as desk chairs in homes and offices, in living rooms, and in opera houses and theaters from Bar Harbor to Sheboygan to Corpus Christi, Aspen, Winnipeg, and Vancouver. Many have survived. In the 1920s, mass-produced versions with plain backs and dowel-rod rungs and spindles were glued together and sold by the millions as kitchen chairs.

The fabric designs on the five kitchen/opera chairs shown in the following pages are patterns derived from the carved decorations in the wood. But their use is not limited to these chairs. They are so contemporary in concept that the designs can be used for most present day chairs as well as for any antique chair that relates well with the forms.

This first kitchen/opera chair belonged to Gail's grandfather, who used it as his desk chair. (Gail is my son John's girl friend.) The design is striking as well as pleasing with the chair rail forms in the back peeking through the engraved forms. Besides needling the seat, Gail gave the chair a bath and lots of rubbing, cleaning, and tender loving care. It shows and was worth every minute of her effort.

Originally a kitchen chair in a Wisconsin farm house, three generations of Gail's family have used it plain. Now, it's in the big city—and fancy.

Figure II-22. Kitchen/opera chair with *Morning Glories and Swirls* design. Worked and owned by Gail Harnett.

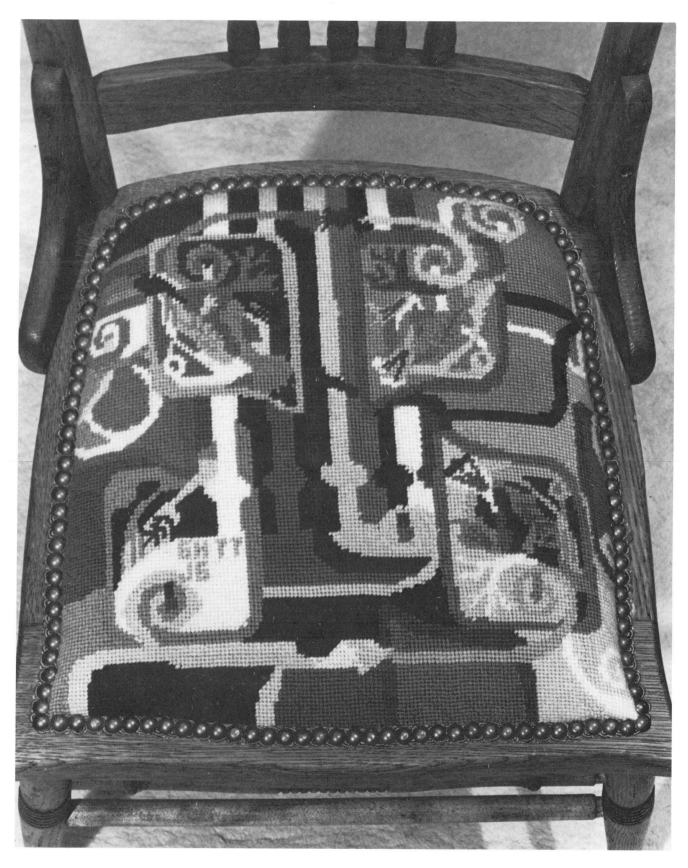

Figure II-23. Detailed view of *Morning Glories and Swirls* design. The seat is 16 inches long and 16½ inches wide (40.6 cm by 41.9 cm).

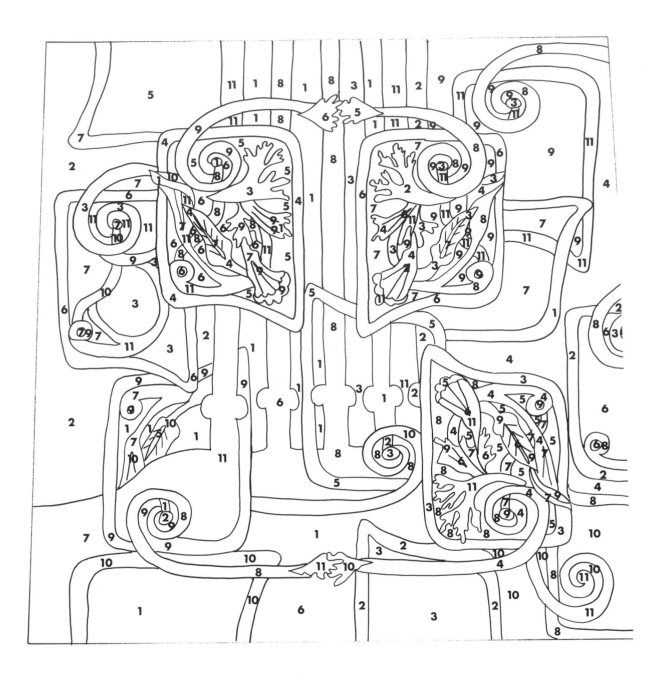

Figure II-24. Color Chart Outline.

Color Guide

Number	Color Name	Paternayan Color
1	dark blue	#311
2	medium dark delft blue	#380
3	medium light delft blue	#381
4	light delft blue	#395
5	dark aqua blue	#750
6	medium dark aqua blue	#755
7	medium light aqua blue	#760
8	light aqua blue	#765
9	medium light pink beige	#133
10	pale beige	#020
11	white	#005

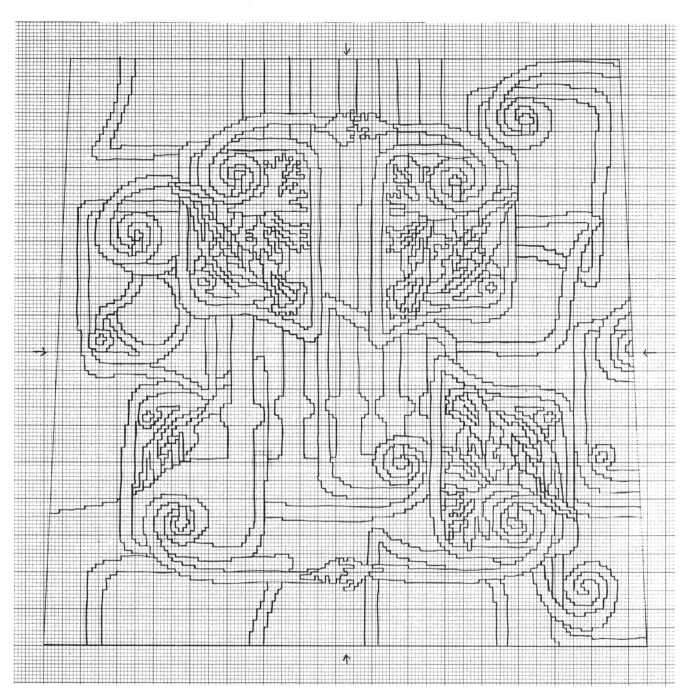

Figure II-25. Graph Outline.

Floral Arabesque

Seat Design (Shown on a Kitchen/Opera Chair)

This chair and the one that follows were found at the student "co-op" at the University of Wisconsin. They were probably turned in to the co-op by students for a tiny bit of cash. For a tiny bit more they were rescued by another student with a designer's eye—my daughter. Susan kept one and let a friend have the other. The chair is now in her home in Washington, D.C. The flowery, stylized arabesque goes with all the houseplants in her brownstone apartment.

Figure II-26. Kitchen/opera chair with *Floral Arabesque* design. Worked and owned by Susan Gross.

Figure II-27. Detailed view of *Floral Arabesque* design. The seat is 14 inches long and 16 inches wide (35.6 cm by 40.6 cm).

Figure II-28. Color Chart Outline.

Color Guide

Number	Color Name	Paternayan Color
1	medium magenta	#644
2	deep purple	#612
3	deep magenta	#221
4	light blue	#382
5	navy blue	#311
6	pale honey beige	#464
7	honey beige	#541

Figure II-29. Graph Outline.

Branches of Leaves

Seat Design (Shown on a Kitchen/Opera Chair)

This chair, also found at the student "co-op" at the University of Wisconsin, has a more delicate look and a simpler, carved design. The carved branch of leaves, which is seen so often in these chairs, was translated almost exactly as the central effect in this design. This chair is oak and I have seen others much like it in hickory and pine.

What was once held so low as to be given away for a few dollars is now highly prized.

Figure II-30. Kitchen/opera chair with *Branches of Leaves* design. Worked and owned by Mrs. Robert M. Eckhouse.

Figure II-31. Detailed view of *Branches of Leaves* design. The size is 15 inches long and 18 inches wide (38.1 cm by 45.7 cm).

Fiqure II-32. Color Chart Outline.

Color Guide

Number	Color Name	Paternayan Color
1	dark aqua blue	#750
2	medium dark aqua blue	#755
3	medium light aqua blue	#760
4	light aqua blue	#765
5	khaki	#521
6	mustard	#440
7	brick	#416
8	orange	#434

Figure II-33. Graph Outline.

Circles and Leaves

Seat Design (Shown on a Kitchen/Opera Chair)

This and the design that follows are based upon the ingenuity of the early American woodcarver. He decorated every chair with a wide variety of clear and forceful designs. Each chair design was slightly different, yet similar. The combination of natural and stylized forms in the chair suggested a less involved design for the seat fabric. These are excellent designs to use when a strong design and simple color palette are needed to temper the fussiness of the chair itself.

Figure II-34. Kitchen/opera chair with *Circles and Leaves* design. Worked and owned by Jean Goldberg.

Figure II-35. Detailed view of *Circles and Leaves* design. The seat is 16 inches long and 15 inches wide (40.6 cm by 38.1 cm).

46

Figure II-36. Color Chart Outline. (The flower petals in
the small circles are the same color within each circle.
The areas inside the small circles are all the same color.)

Color Guide

Number	Color Name	Paternayan Color	Number	Color Name	Paternayan Color
1	dark lemon orange	#960	8	lemon yellow	#450
2	medium dark lemon orange	#965	9	light yellow	#438
3	medium light lemon orange	#970	10	dark brown	#114
4	light lemon orange	#975	11	medium dark brown	#124
5	dark gold	#427	12	medium light brown	#134
6	medium dark gold	#440	13	light brown	#136
7	yellow	#442	14	beige	#020

Figure II-37. Graph Outline.

Victorian Fans

Seat Design (Shown on a Kitchen/Opera Chair)

When a chair boasts a variety of abstract designs, making a simplified variation of those designs for the seat design is a fine idea. The carvings in this type of chair are often so active that neutral colors are necessary in order to mute the chair's activity.

Figure II-38. Kitchen/opera chair with *Victorian Fans* design. Worked and owned by Jean Goldberg.

Figure II-39. Detailed view of *Victorian Fans* design. The seat is 16 inches long and 15 inches wide (40.6 cm by 38.1 cm).

Figure II-40. Color Chart Outline. (The double-circled dot forms are the same color within each spray. The areas around the dots are all the same color.)

Color Guide

Number	Color Name	Paternayan Color	Number	Color Name	Paternayan Color
1	dark tile	#414	7	pale orange	#464
2	medium dark tile	#416	8	dark red orange	#958
3	dark orange	#424	9	red orange	#968
4	medium dark orange	#434	10	medium red orange	#978
5	medium light orange	#444	11	dark gold	#427
6	light orange	#454	12	gold	#447

Figure II-41. Graph Outline.

Roses and Swirls

Seat and Back Design (Shown on an All-American Rocker)

Rockers are a great American happening. They were born in America and grew up here. Benjamin Franklin had rockers put on one of his chairs; it has not been proven, but it is strongly suspected that the rocker was his invention. President Abraham Lincoln was assassinated while sitting in a rocker at Ford's Theater in Washington, D.C., and that style of rocker became identified by his name. President John F. Kennedy's rocker became world famous and gave new strength to the rocker-making industry.

(text continued on page 56)

Figure II-42. All-American rocker with *Roses and Swirls* design. Worked by Bunny Factor. Chair owned by Pat Cohen.

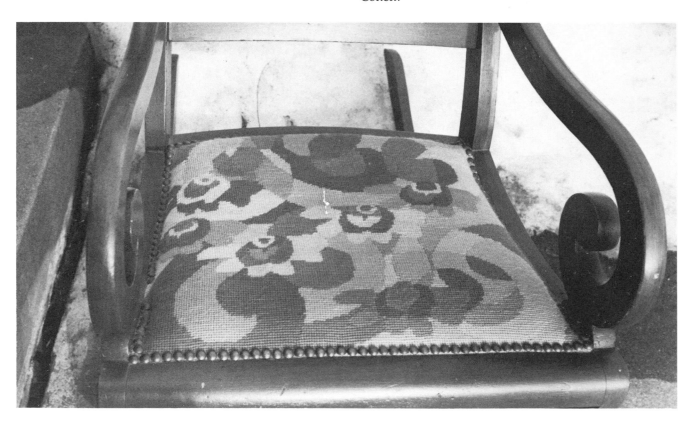

Figure II-43. Detailed view of *Roses and Swirls* design on seat. The seat is 25 inches long and 24 inches wide (63.5 cm by 70 cm).

Figure II-44. Detailed view of *Roses and Swirls* design on back.

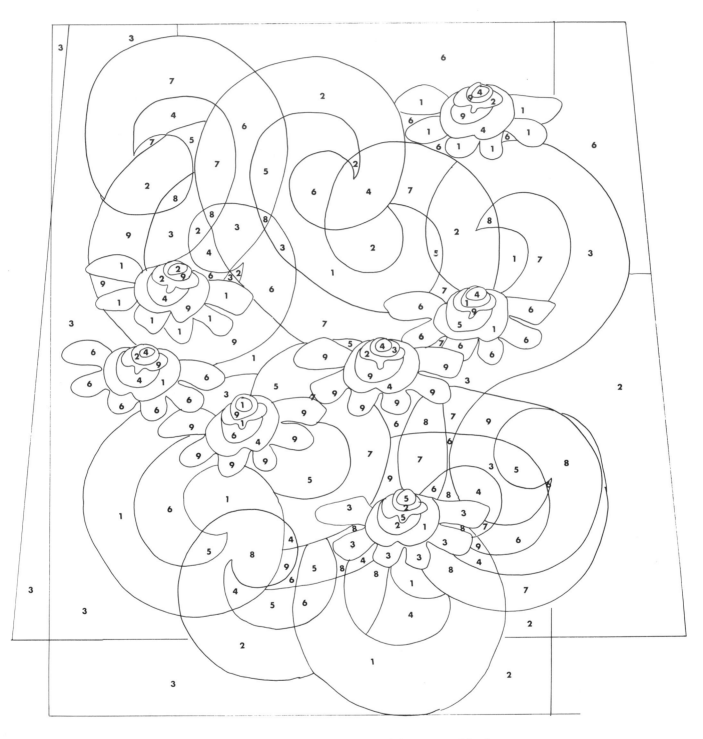

Figure II-45. Color Chart Outline. (The seat and back
have overlapping outlines.)

Color Guide

Number	Color Name	Paternayan Color	Number	Color Name	Paternayan Color
1	dark orange	#424	6	yellow	#457
2	orange	#434	7	medium light yellow	#442
3	light orange	#444	8	light yellow	#437
4	dark yellow	#427	9	pale yellow	#438
5	medium dark yellow	#447			

54

Figure ll-46. Graph Outline.

As early as the late 1700s, Europeans proudly displayed any rocker that came from America. To this day the rocker is the simple comfort chair of our country and is now enjoyed around the world.

This rocker was bought to rock a first grand-child in; to feed him and to soothe him. I helped the grandmother find it at an antique shop. The grandfather refinished the chair and I designed the cover to go with it. Grandmother stitched the covering. The curlique shape of the arm became the basis of the pattern and the roses and leaves were the focus decoration. You can see how the seat and back were lifted from the same design. Notice that the Graph Outline and the Color Chart Outline are marked to show both pieces. You can take your measurements and use what you need for your chair.

Oriental Colors

Seat Design (Shown on an English Rocker)

The chair seat on this nursing rocker was done in colors to match an Oriental rug. The English rocker is a smiling accompaniment to the bed-room where it resides. The design forms are de-rived from the rocker's curliques and knobs. They are humorous and fun-loving and can be used for many a chair. The chair was brought from Scotland and was used three generations ago to nurse this new baby's grandmother.

Figure II-47. English rocker with *Oriental Colors.* The seat is 14 inches long and 17 inches wide (35.6 cm by 43.2 cm). Worked and owned by Rita C. Sachs.

Figure II-48. Color Chart Outline.

Color Guide

Number	Color Name	Paternayan Color
1	gold	#521
2	light honey beige	#455
3	greyed pink	#281
4	maroon	#207
5	medium delft blue	#380
6	medium dark delft blue	#314
7	dark green	#528

Figure II-49. Graph Outline.

Swirling Leaves

Seat Design (Shown on a Fancy Rocker)

As you would expect, some American furniture makers in the nineteenth and early twentieth century went all out with decorative carvings. The design on this seat was derived from the carvings on the chair which provided both small and large elements to contrast with each other. The neutral colors have a softening effect on the bold, ornate decorations in the wood.

Figure II-50. Fancy rocker with *Swirling Leaves* design. Worked and owned by Jean Goldberg.

Figure II-51. Detailed view of *Swirling Leaves* design. The seat is 26 inches long and 20 inches wide (66 cm by 50.8 cm).

Color Guide

Number	Color Name	Paternayan Color	Number	Color Name	Paternayan Color
1	dark yellow	#427	7	pale honey beige	#455
2	medium dark yellow	#440	8	dark khaki	#521
3	pale yellow	#438	9	medium light khaki	#531
4	pale greyed yellow	#040	10	light khaki	#541
5	dark gold	#433	11	medium greyed brown	#134
6	gold	#445	12	medium light greyed brown	#136

Figure II-52. Color Chart Outline. (The double-circled dot forms are the same color within each row. The areas around the dots are all the same color.)

Figure II-53. Graph Outline.

62

Circles in Motion

Chair-Pad Design (Shown on Two Windsor Chairs)

While the same pattern was used for both chairs in this pair of Windsors, the colors in each chair are in different relationships. The darks and lights change positions in each chair. The pattern itself was developed from the circular forms in the chairs. Some nice, tight decorative stitches are used in these seat pads, too. The stitches are designated so that you can try them and the diagrams and instructions for these stitches can be found in Part I.

Figure II-54. Full-length view of Windsor chair.

Figure II-55. Pair of Windsor chairs with *Circles in Motion* design. Worked by Janis Bente. Chairs owned by Mr. and Mrs. James Bente.

These chairs, owned by friends, are part of a set consisting of the two armchairs shown and four matching side chairs. They are from the Beacon Hill Collection, reproduced in the 1920s from the original Philadelphia comb-back chairs of circa 1765.

Figure II-56. Detailed view of *Circles in Motion* design. The seat is 17 inches long and 23½ inches wide (43.2 cm by 59.7 cm).

When it was brought to America, the English Windsor chair was a heavy, strong chair. The American version was lighter and easier to handle. The Windsor was thought to be the first comfortable, all-wood chair in America. It has a broad saddle seat, slightly stilted back, and there are many versions. This one is a comb-back.

Light-and-Dark Color Guide

Number	Color Name	Paternayan Color
1	yellow	#442
2	medium light yellow	#437
3	pale yellow	#438
4	pale greyed yellow	#040
5	pale green	#593
6	dark aqua blue	#750
7	medium dark aqua blue	#755
8	medium dark delft blue	#380
9	medium light delft blue	#381
10	medium dark greyed green	#553
11	medium dark yellow green	#545
12	medium light yellow green	#550
13	medium light greyed green	#590

Dark-and-Light Color Guide

Number	Color Name	Paternayan Color
1	dark aqua blue	#750
2	medium dark aqua blue	#755
3	medium dark delft blue	#380
4	medium light delft blue	#381
5	medium dark greyed green	#553
6	medium light greyed green	#590
7	pale green	#593
8	medium dark yellow green	#545
9	medium light yellow green	#550
10	yellow	#442
11	medium light yellow	#437
12	pale yellow	#438
13	greyed pale yellow	#040

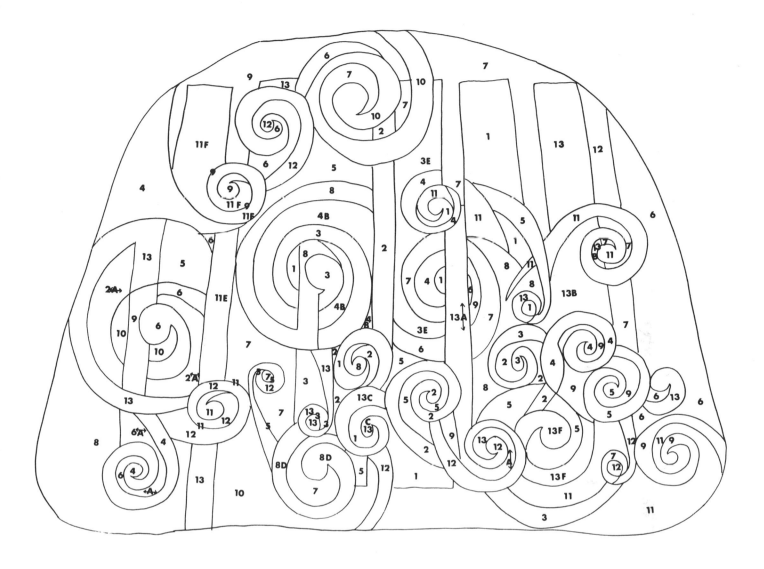

Figure II-57. Color Chart Outline. (A number imposed
directly on a line indicates that the line is to be done in
that color.)

Stitch Guide

Letter	Stitch Name	Stitch Direction
A	oblong cross	↔ or ↕
B	knotted stitch	
C	kalem stitch	
D	knitting stitch	
E	mosaic stitch	
F	interlocking gobelin	

Figure II-58. Graph Outline.

Part III

PATTERNS FOR ANY CHAIR

My first introduction to making chair seat designs was with old chairs, but I soon discovered that many of the patterns I had created were suitable for contemporary chairs. These patterns, which I had lifted from the carvings on antique chairs, looked so good on contemporary chairs because antique chair shapes and carvings are largely adaptations from nature. They are appropriate for antique, contemporary, or avant-garde modern forms, so long as their colors are controlled. Having learned that the natural forms work quite well on any chair, I began to use everything around me as an inspiration for design—leaves, outside and inside, stylized and natural, snowflakes, manhole covers, children's hands and feet, names and dates, flowers, circles. These patterns are contemporary whether they are used on new or old chairs.

Elm, Maple, and Locust Leaves

**Seat Design (Shown on a Spindle Chair
and a Victorian Side Chair)**

Leaf patterns are wonderful in almost any room. They are almost like an indoor garden. Patterns can be subtle and will not fight with your plants. Color will determine the boldness and striking visual impression of the chair seat. The same pattern can be subdued or striking, depending on the colors used. The colors in this pattern of leaves from the yard, traced and arranged in a pleasant, integrated mass, were not bound by nature. Instead, they are inventive and playful.

This pattern is a good example of one design that is appropriate for different types of chairs. The light and delicate spindle chair (shown in Figure III-1), which is a less sturdy version of a Shaker design, is exactly right for the elm, maple, and locust leaf pattern. Its light background and subtle colors brighten what started out originally as a drab, rather nondescript example of an occasional chair.

The sturdy Victorian chair (shown in Figure

Figure III-1. The *Elm, Maple, and Locust Leaves* design worked with a light background. Worked and owned by Judith Gross.

Figure III-2. The *Elm, Maple, and Locust Leaves* design worked with a dark background. Worked and owned by Mrs. Robert M. Eckhouse.

III-2) was new in a small midwestern town about seventy-five to eighty years ago. It needed just a bit of rehabilitation and the integrity of the fabric's dark background with its light leaves to become a prized and useful piece of art.

Figure III-3. Detailed view of the *Elm, Maple, and Locust Leaves* design. The seat is 17 inches long and 17 inches wide (43.2 cm by 43.2 cm).

Figure III-4. Color Chart Outline. (A number imposed directly on a line indicates that the line is to be done in that color.)

Light Background Color Guide

Number	Color Name	Paternayan Color
1	dark khaki	#511
2	medium blue	#380
3	tile	#416
4	orange	#427
5	coral orange	#426
6	honey beige	#541

Dark Background Color Guide

Number	Color Name	Paternayan Color
1	dark khaki	#511
2	medium blue	#380
3	tile	#416
4	orange	#427
5	coral orange	#426
6	mauve	#123

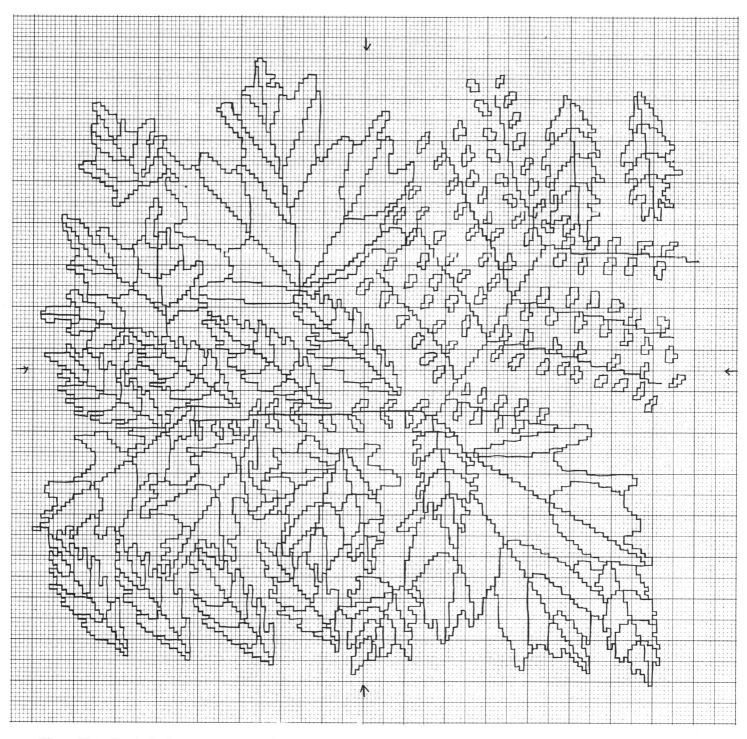

Figure III-5. Graph Outline.

Split-Leaf Philodendra

Chair-Pad Design (Shown on a Kitchen Windsor Chair)

Just as one design can be versatile, so can one set of colors work together so well that they can be used in a number of related designs. You'll notice that the same colors were used in the four chair-pad designs that follow. The harmony of the colors and basic idea behind all four designs may stimulate you to liven up any room with these houseplant leaf fabrics. (That is, they are houseplants unless you live in the tropics!) The designs can be used for pads, seats, and backs.

While I love both types of philodendra, the wonderful cutouts and folds of the split-leaf are full of many ins-and-outs. It its own way each leaf reminds me of the human hand, itself a perfect basis for design.

Figure III-6. Split-Leaf Philodendra design. Worked and owned by Gail Harnett.

Figure III-7. Detail of *Split-Leaf Philodendra* design. The chair pad is 16 inches long and 17 inches wide (40.6 cm by 43.2 cm).

Figure III-8. Color Chart Outline. (A number imposed directly on a line indicates that the line is to be done in that color.)

Color Guide

Number	Color Name	Paternayan Color	Number	Color Name	Paternayan Color
1	medium dark tile orange	#416	7	medium light khaki	#445
2	medium light tile orange	#426	8	light khaki	#541
3	light tile orange	#425	9	pale khaki	#015
4	light orange	#454	10	medium light pink beige	#249
5	dark khaki	#521	11	light pink beige	#271
6	dark gold	#433	12	pale beige	#020

Figure III-9. Graph Outline.

74

Schefflera Leaves

**Chair-Pad Design (Shown on a Kitchen
Windsor Chair)**

After photographing my schefflera plant from
every possible angle, I made a photo-montage
and used it as the basis for this botanical design.
The little design elements scattered throughout
the space make it interesting to work.

Figure III-10. Schefflera Leaves design. The chair pad is 16
inches long and 17 inches wide (40.6 cm by 43.2 cm).
Worked and owned by Gail Harnett.

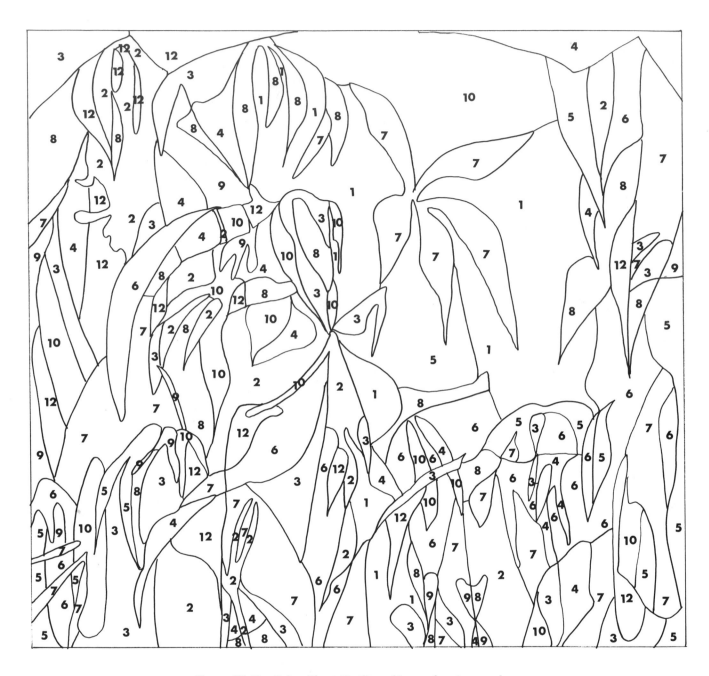

Figure III-11. Color Chart Outline. (A number imposed directly on a line indicates that the line is to be done in that color.)

Color Guide

Number	Color Name	Paternayan Color	Number	Color Name	Paternayan Color
1	medium dark tile orange	#416	7	medium light khaki	#445
2	medium light tile orange	#426	8	light khaki	#541
3	light tile orange	#425	9	pale khaki	#015
4	light orange	#454	10	medium light pink beige	#249
5	dark khaki	#521	11	light pink beige	#271
6	dark gold	#433	12	pale beige	#020

76

Figure III-12. Graph Outline.

Fern Fronds

Chair-Pad Design (Shown on a Kitchen Windsor Chair)

In nature the leaves of ferns make a pattern of small elements that are universally appealing. In this design their arrangement is bold and striking so that the fabric becomes highly decorative.

Figure III-13. Fern Fronds design. The chair pad is 16 inches long and 17 inches wide (40.6 cm by 43.2 cm). Worked and owned by Gail Harnett.

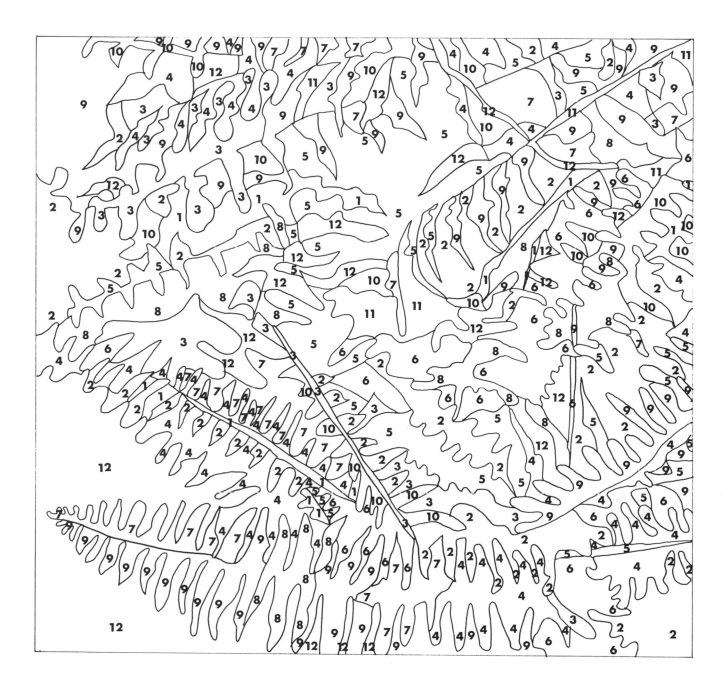

Figure III-14. Color Chart Outline. (A number imposed directly on a line indicates that the line is to be done in that color.)

Color Guide

Number	Color Name	Paternayan Color	Number	Color Name	Paternayan Color
1	medium dark tile orange	#416	7	medium light khaki	#445
2	medium light tile orange	#426	8	light khaki	#541
3	light tile orange	#425	9	pale khaki	#015
4	light orange	#454	10	medium light pink beige	#249
5	dark khaki	#521	11	light pink beige	#271
6	dark gold	#433	12	pale beige	#020

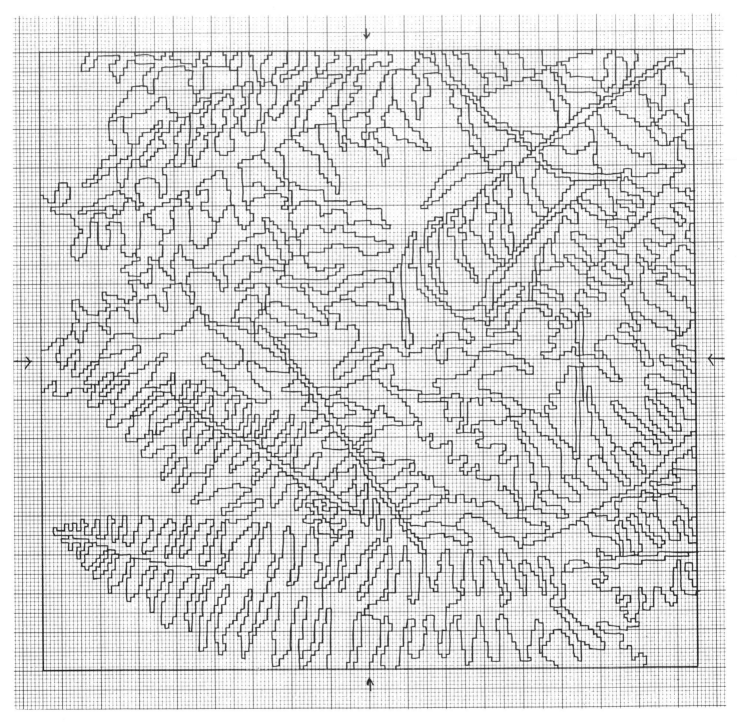

Figure III-15. Graph Outline.

Joya Vine

Chair-Pad Design (Shown on a Kitchen Windsor Chair)

With a vine that hangs and climbs, you can create a perfectly natural all-over design. The many-shaded joya leaf adds lights and darks that are interesting to work and enjoyable to view when completed.

Figure III-16. Joya Vine design. The chair pad is 16 inches long and 17 inches wide (40.6 cm by 43.2 cm). Worked and owned by Gail Harnett.

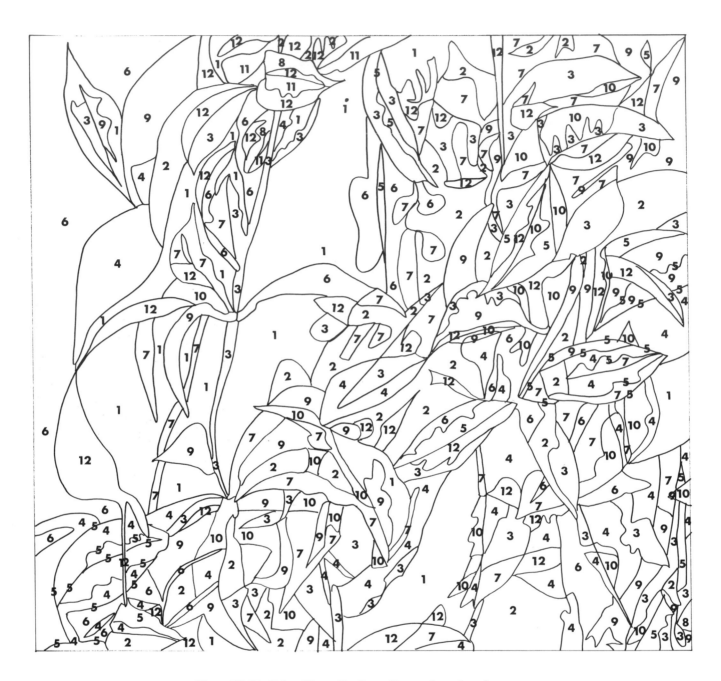

Figure III-17. Color Chart Outline. (A number placed directly on a line indicates that the line is to be done in that color.)

Color Guide

Number	Color Name	Paternayan Color	Number	Color Name	Paternayan Color
1	medium dark tile orange	#416	7	medium light khaki	#445
2	medium light tile orange	#426	8	light khaki	#541
3	light tile orange	#425	9	pale khaki	#015
4	light orange	#454	10	medium light pink beige	#249
5	dark khaki	#521	11	light pink beige	#271
6	dark gold	#433	12	pale beige	#020

82

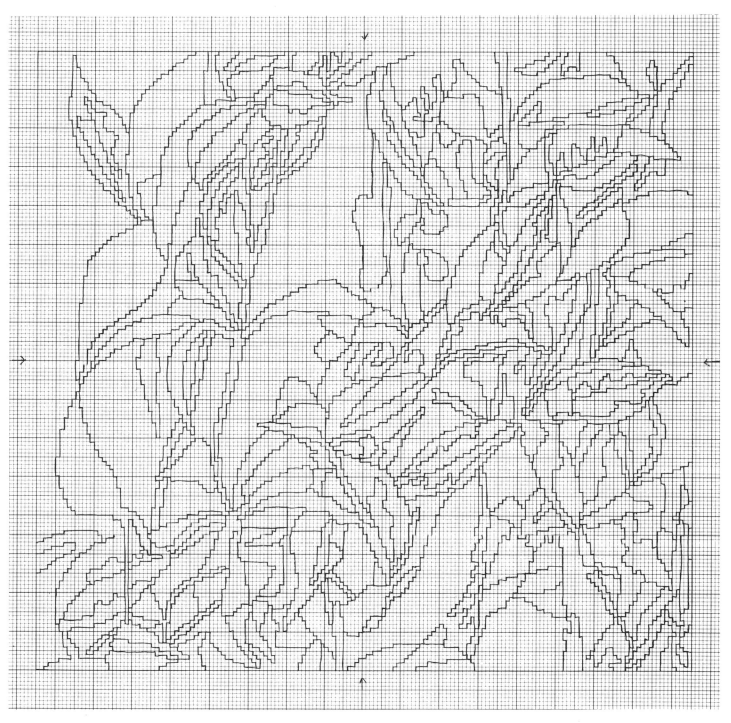

Figure III-18. Graph Outline.

Snowflakes

Piano- or Chair-Pad Design (Shown on a Piano Bench, a Contemporary Bentwood Chair, and a Heart-Shaped-Back Chair)

Perhaps because all living things repeat themselves in similar form from generation to generation, human beings are often pleased with repetitive designs. They provide a sense of order even when the repetition is a little inexact, as is nature. So, there is an important place for repeated patterns in fabrics for the wall, floor, and furniture.

The snowflake pattern shown here is one I have worked for several seating needs—a Bentwood chair, a piano bench, and a chair with a heart-shaped back. I was given quite a thrill when, walking through the King Tut Show at the Field Museum in Chicago, I saw a stool from his pyramid. Its pattern had a feeling so similar to the snowflakes I had been making for the past ten years that I laughed out loud. I had known for a long time that nothing really is new, just seen again by new eyes and reinterpreted. But so long ago!

The pictured chairs show an inventive use of forms, added as wanted and needed to fill in the space. You have all the ingredients to fit any space you want to cover. Just follow the directions in Part I. Place the design in consecutive order to achieve the yardage you need for your chair or bench. Add as much of the second part of the design as you need.

Figure III-19. Snowflakes design on piano bench. Worked and owned by Anita Goldberg.

Figure III-20. Snowflakes design on Bentwood chair.
Worked by Elsa Mond. Chair owned by Dr. and Mrs.
Ernest Mond.

Figure III-21. Snowflakes design on heart-shaped-back chair. Worked by Judith Gross. Chair owned by Mr. and Mrs. Morton J. Harris.

Figure III-22. Detail of *Snowflakes* design on Bentwood chair.

Figure III-23. Detail of *Snowflakes* design on heart-shaped-back chair.

Piano Bench Color Guide

Number	Color Name	Paternayan Color
1	khaki	#136
2	medium royal blue	#731
3	light honey beige	#453
4	yellow	#441
5	medium yellow	#442
6	navy blue	#311
7	dark yellow	#427

Figure III-24. Color Chart Outline.

Bentwood Chair Color Guide

Number	Color Name	Paternayan Color
1	dark green	#540
2	light brick	#426
3	pale honey beige	#455
4	mauve	#123
5	medium dark green	#553
6	dark brick	#416
7	light honey beige	#453

Heart-Shaped-Back Color Guide

Number	Color Name	Paternayan Color
1	dark green	#540
2	light khaki	#541
3	gold	#440
4	dark orange	#424
5	medium yellow green	#545
6	light yellow	#442
7	light orange	#444

Figure III-25. Graph Outline.

Formal Leaves

Seat Design (Shown on a Chippendale Chair)

A stylized leaf is used in this design in an all-over pattern. The colors create the visual excitement that makes this chair seat pattern so pleasing. I have shown two color suggestions here, but you can combine your own color choices. Figure III-29 will show you how to add horizontally or vertically to the design to fit any seating need.

Figure III-26. Detailed view of *Formal Leaves* design in Frank. Chair owned by Dr. and Mrs. Richard Burnstine.

Figure III-27. Detailed view of *Formal Leaves* deisgn in reds, oranges, neutrals, and navy color scheme. The seat is 15 inches long and 25 inches wide (38.1 cm by 63.5 cm).

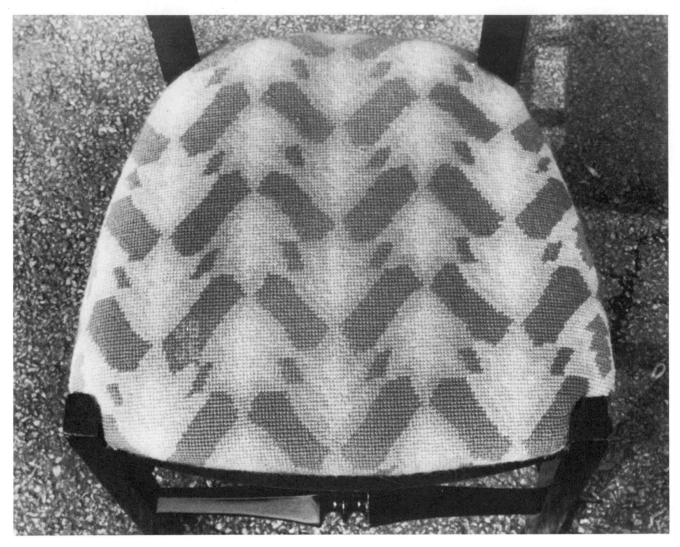

Figure III-28. Detailed view of *Formal Leaves* design in yellows, golds, and white color scheme. Worked and owned by Mrs. Edward G. Bazelon.

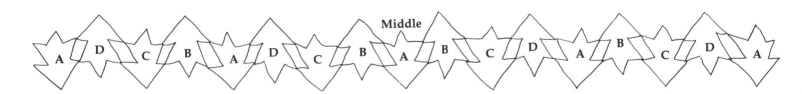

Figure III-29. Diagram for repeating pattern. There are nine forms horizontally in this design as it is shown in the photographs. The color relationships in the nine forms are marked by letters. The middle form is A and spanning out on both sides of A the color relationships are:

A D C B—A—B C D A
Additional forms can be done by adding A D C B (to the left) of the middle A and B C D A (to the right) of the middle A, horizontally, as large as you wish. Use the same basic procedure to add more rows vertically, if necessary.

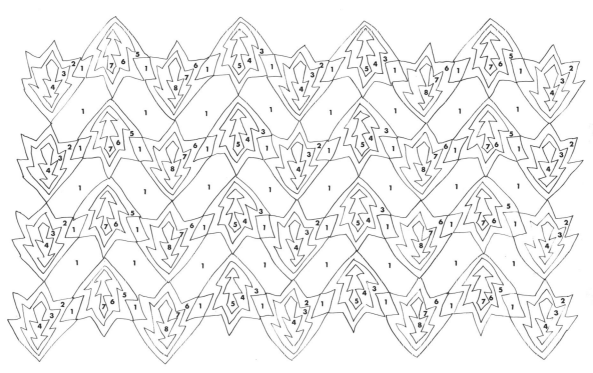

Figure III-30. Color Chart Outline.

Yellow-Gold-White Color Guide

Number	Color Name	Paternayan Color
1	dark yellow	#427
2	medium dark yellow	#440
3	yellow	#441
4	medium light yellow	#442
5	light yellow	#438
6	medium pale yellow	#458
7	pale yellow	#468
8	white	#005

Red-Orange-Navy Color Guide

Number	Color Name	Paternayan Color
1	navy blue	#311
2	dark maroon	#207
3	dark red	#240
4	bright red	#242
5	orange red	#958
6	medium light greyed beige	#132
7	light beige	#138
8	pale beige	#020

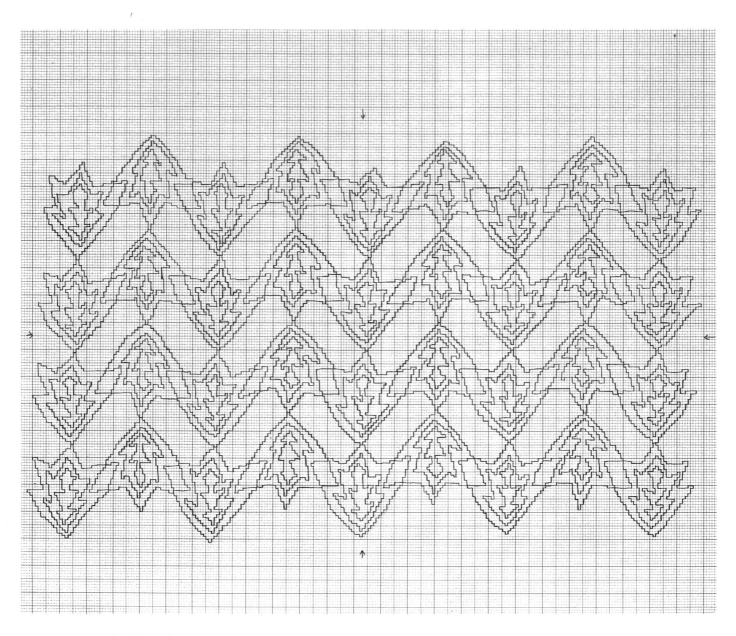

Figure III-31. Graph Outline.

Formal Victorian

Seat and Back Design (Shown on a Victorian Chair)

You can use this pattern with four shades of any color, from dark to light, and repeat the patterns to fit any size. Figure III-34 will show you how to increase or decrease the pattern as needed.

Figure III-32. Formal Victorian design. The seat is 22 inches long and 18 inches wide (55.9 cm by 45.7 cm). Worked by Rita C. Sachs, Barbara Sachs Linn, and Laurie Sachs. Chair owned by·Rita and Sam Sachs.

Figure III-33. Color Chart Outline. (A number imposed directly on a line indicates that the line is to be done in that color.)

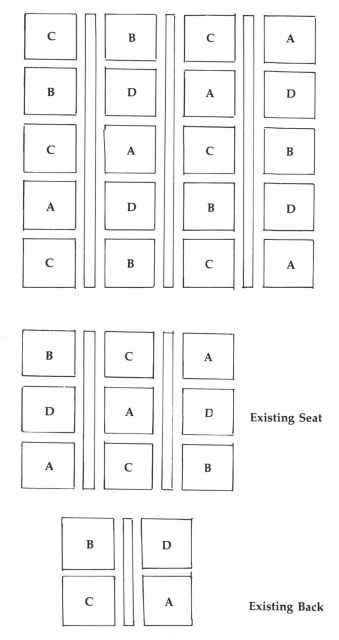

Figure III-34. Diagram for repeating pattern. Each letter designates the colors used within the area marked. There are four different color relationships, which are designated by the letters A B C D. The seat and back are marked. The larger diagram shows how to increase and expand the patterns as needed. You can choose any four colors to use this pattern successfully.

Color Guide

Number	Color Name	Paternayan Color
1	dark aqua blue	#750
2	medium dark aqua blue	#755
3	medium light aqua blue	#760
4	light aqua blue	#765

Figure III-35. Graph Outline.

Grapes and Leaves

**Seat and Back Design (Shown on a
Queen-Anne-Type Chair)**

This pattern was developed with the leaf pattern and the grape designs used again and again. Decorative stitchery was added in some tight stitches for textures. While a chair is done best in plain basketweave for durability, there are some tight stitches that don't catch or pull and are good and wearable for chairs. I have designated the stitches with letters, as well as the colors by numbers. A chart for doing these stitches can be found in Part I.

The explanation for how to take the parts of this chair from the largest part of the design, the seat, can also be found in Part I, and you can get the pieces you need for your chair the same way.

Figure III-36. Grapes and Leaves design. Worked and owned by Mrs. Robert M. Eckhouse.

Figure III-37. View of Grapes and Leaves design on back.

Figure III-38. Detailed view of *Grapes and Leaves* design on seat. The seat is 24 inches long and 24 inches wide (61 cm by 61 cm).

Color Guide

Number	Color Name	Paternayan Color
1	navy blue	#311
2	dark royal blue	#721
3	medium royal blue	#731
4	medium hyacinth blue	#621
5	light blue	#743
6	light greyed blue	#382
7	medium dark greyed blue	#143
8	dark hyacinth blue	#642
9	dark maroon purple	#612
10	light hyacinth blue	#631
11	pale greyed blue	#017
12	white	#005
13	dark aqua blue	#750
14	medium dark aqua blue	#755
15	medium light aqua blue	#760
16	light aqua blue	#765

Stitch Guide

Letter	Stitch Name	Stitch Direction
A	kalem stitch	
B	knotted stitch	
C	interlocking gobelin	
D	oblong cross	↔ or ↕
E	mosaic stitch	
F	cashmere stitch	

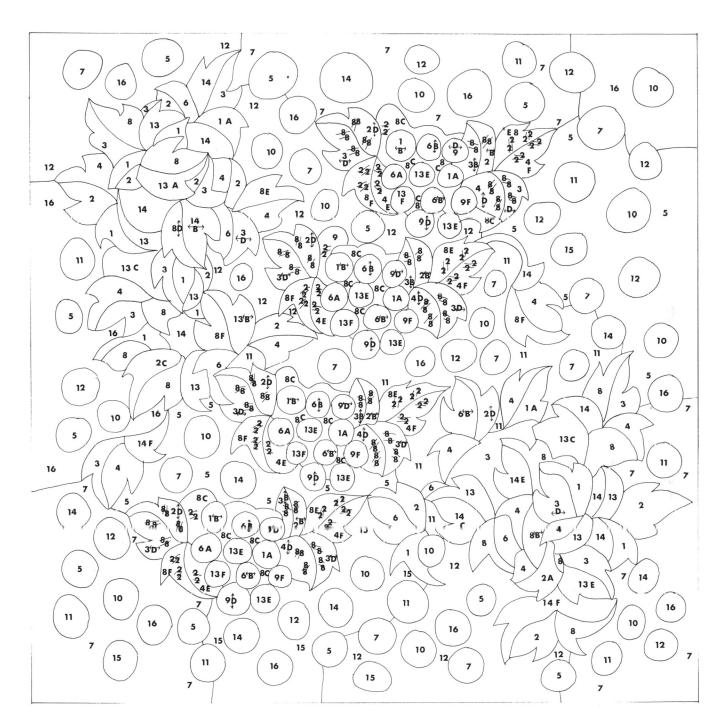

Figure III-39. Color Chart Outline. (A number imposed directly on a line indicates that the line is to be done in that color.)

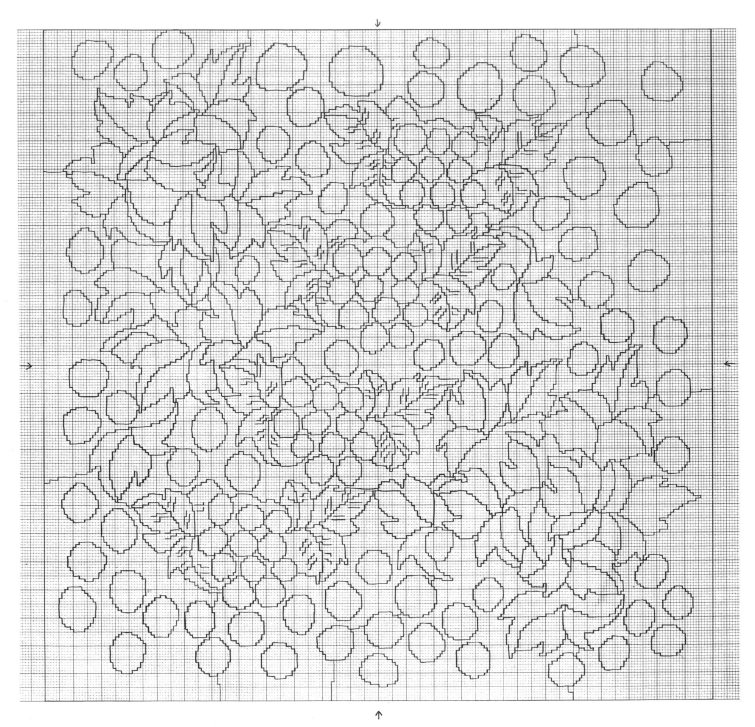

Figure III-40. Graph Outline.

Manhole Covers

Chair-Pad Design (Shown on a Contemporary Windsor Chair)

This pattern represents a truly contemporary use of an old object—manhole covers. This man-made form, from a necessary and essential need, was the inspiration for the chair cover. It has as much beauty as a natural form and although it is utilitarian, it is well designed. The round and square forms were worked together in a galaxy of oranges and neutral shades. This design is a good complement to all kinds of chairs. This particular chair is a modern Scandinavian adaptation of a Windsor chair.

Figure III-41. Manhole Covers design. Owned and worked by Carol Solomon.

Figure III-42. Detailed view of *Manhole Covers* design. The pad is 17½ inches long and 23½ inches wide (44.5 cm by 59.7 cm).

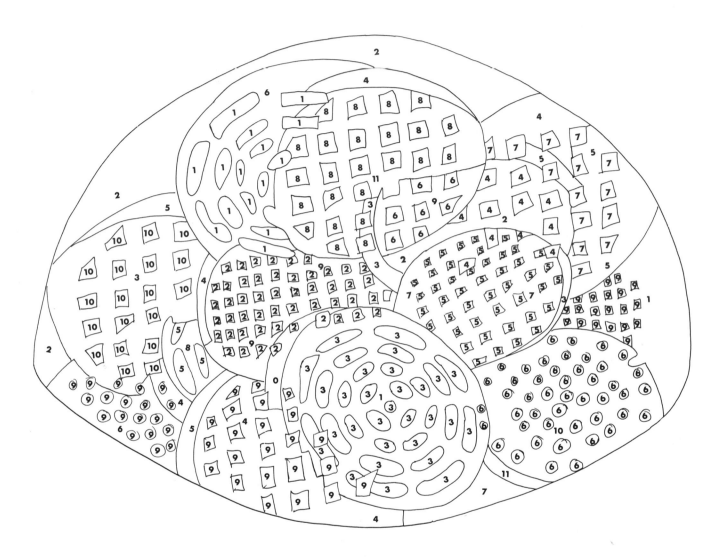

Figure III-43. Color Chart Outline.

Color Guide

Number	Color Name	Paternayan Color
1	dark brick	#414
2	brick	#416
3	dark orange	#424
4	orange	#434
5	red orange	#958
6	medium dark yellow	#440
7	yellow	#441
8	medium light yellow	#437
9	medium light orange	#444
10	light brick	#454
11	pale orange	#464

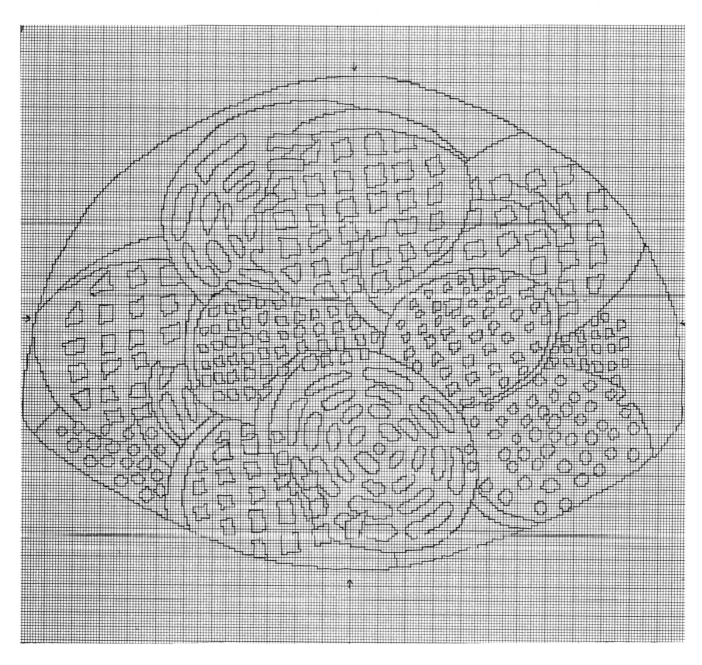

Figure III-44. Graph Outline.

Hands and Feet

Seat Design (Shown on a Bentwood Child's Chair)

This Bentwood child's chair has a pad with a small child's hands and feet, as well as with ABC's and 123's scattered throughout. Your own child's name or initials can be added or substituted. Just use the alphabet in Figure III-69 if you don't care to design letters of your own.

Figure III-45. Hands and Feet design. Worked and owned by Judith Gross.

Figure III-46. Detail of *Hands and Feet* design. The pad is 14¾ inches (37.5 cm) in diameter.

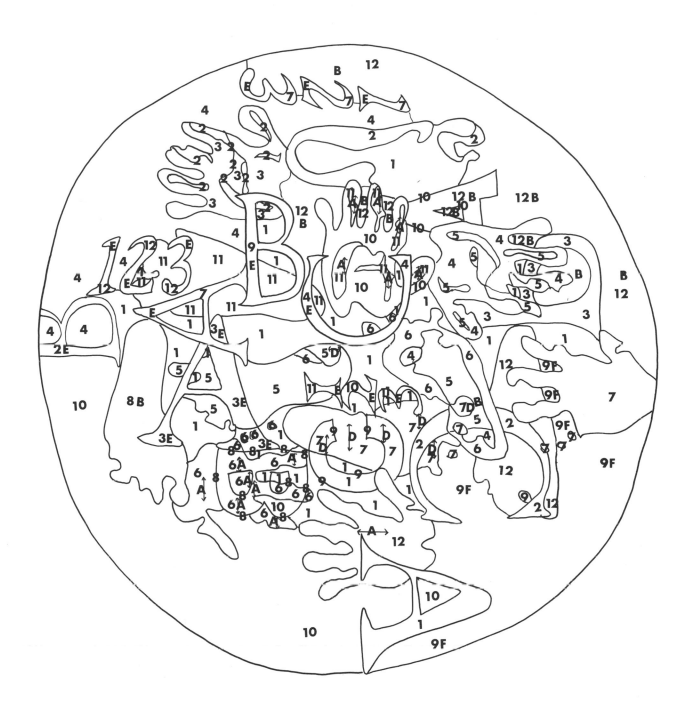

Color Guide

Number	Color Name	Paternayan Color
1	red	#R50
2	dark orange	#958
3	orange	#965
4	dark yellow	#441
5	yellow	#442
6	light yellow	#450
7	bright green	#569
8	dark royal blue	#731
9	royal blue	#721
10	purple	#650
11	light purple	#652
12	white	#005

Figure III-47. Color Chart Outline. (A number imposed directly on a line indicates that the line is to be done in that color.)

Stitch Guide

Letter	Stitch Name	Stitch Direction
A	oblong cross	↔ or ↕
B	mosaic stitch	
C	cashmere stitch	
D	knotted stitch	↔ or ↕
E	interlocking gobelin	
F	kalem stitch	

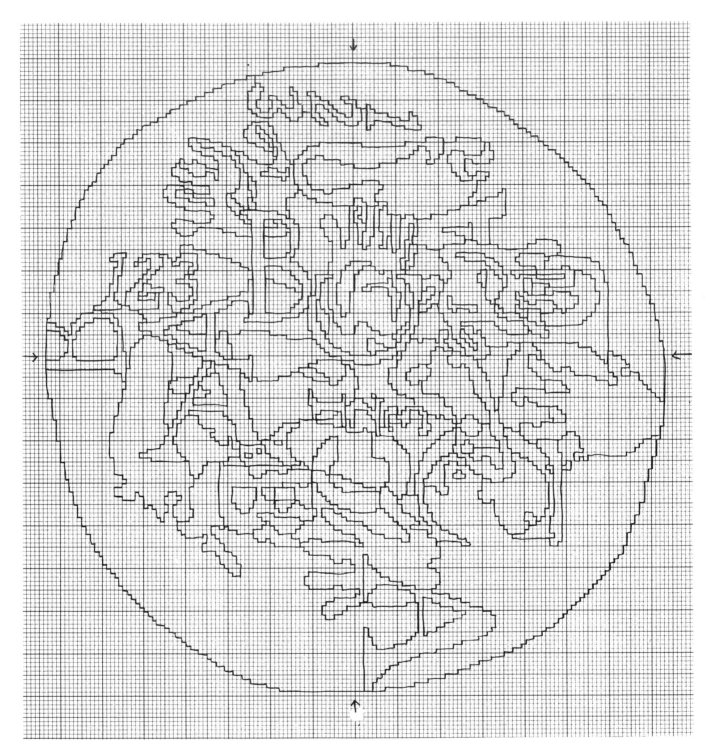

Figure III-48. Graph Outline.

Name and Birthdate

Chair-Pad Design (Shown on a Child's Rocker)

When I was expecting my first grandchild, I began to comb the Pennsylvania countryside where I was living for a suitable rocker. I had helped other grandmothers before in their searches for chairs for their grandchildren. Finally, in the Lancaster area I found this little rocker and Grandpa started to give it the spit and polish his new grandson deserved.

The design has Alex's name and birthdate on it in the pictured chair. I have worked the design in a plain form for you to follow. At the end of this chapter, there is an alphabet and a set of numbers (Figure III-69) to use which will personalize your chair pad for whomever you are making it. You can put your name, the child's name, and birthdate on the design.

Figure III-49. Name and Birthdate design. Worked by Judith Gross. Chair owned by Alex Gross.

Figure III-50. Detailed view of *Name and Birthdate* design. The pad is 13 inches long and 14 inches wide (33 cm by 35.6 cm).

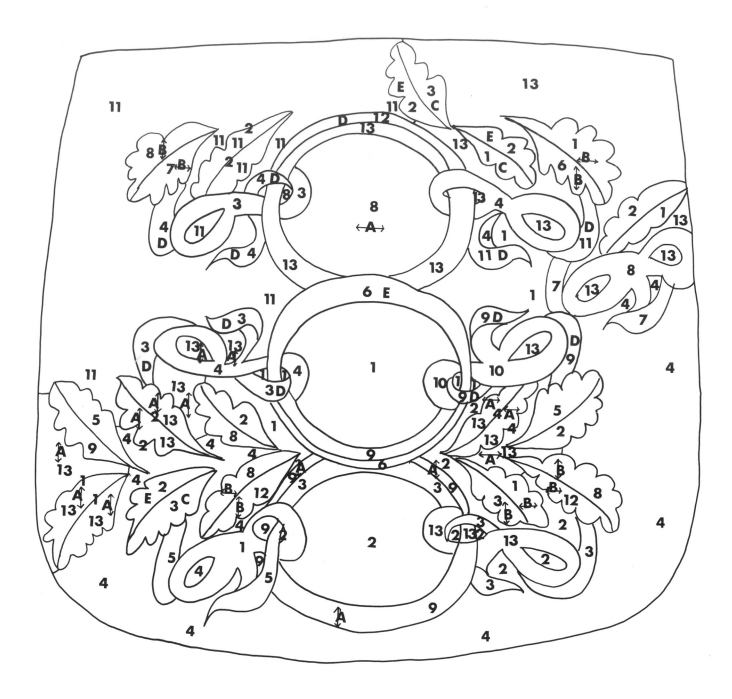

Color Guide

Number	Color Name	Paternayan Color
1	dark navy blue	#311
2	medium dark blue	#314
3	medium light blue	#380
4	light blue	#396
5	dark brown	#124
6	medium dark brown	#134
7	medium light brown	#136
8	pale beige	#020
9	red brown khaki	#126
10	medium light honey	#462
11	light honey	#492
12	pale honey	#011
13	white	#005

Figure III-51. Color Chart Outline. (A number imposed directly on a line indicates that the line is to be done in that color.)

Stitch Guide

Letter	Stitch Name	Stitch Direction
A	oblong cross	↔ or ↕
B	knotted stitch	↔ or ↕
C	kalem stitch	
D	interlocking gobelin	
E	knitting stitch	

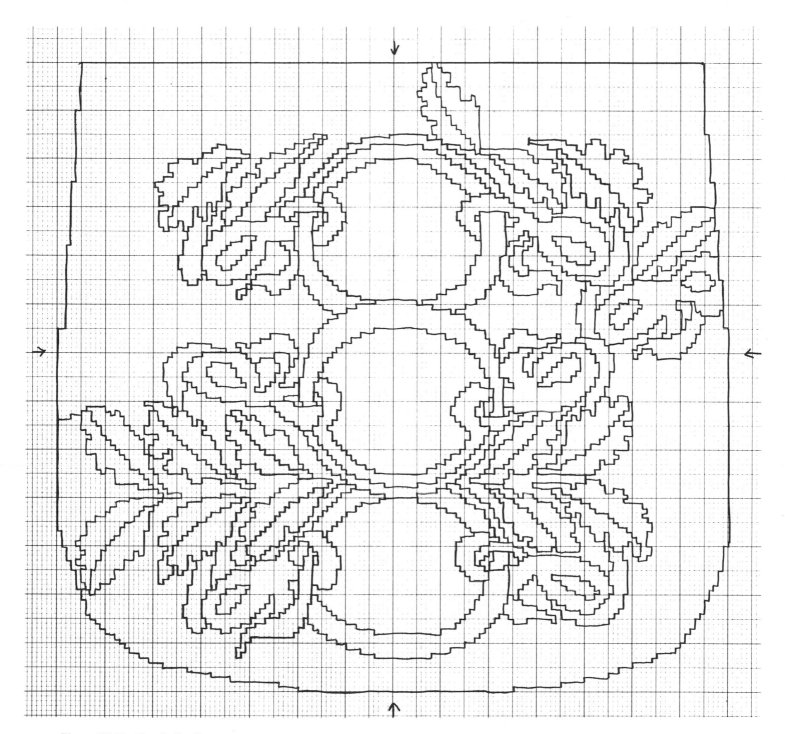

Figure III-52. Graph Outline.

Small Leaves

Chair-Pad Design (Shown on a Child's Rocker)

This design features small leaves for a small girl. The delicate leaf pattern was lifted from the carving on the chair.

Figure III-53. Small Leaves design. Worked by Bunny Factor. Chair owned by Tina Cohen.

Figure III-54. Detailed view of *Small Leaves* design. The pad is 14 inches long and 16 inches wide (35.6 cm by 40.6 cm).

Figure III-55. Color Chart Outline. (A number imposed
directly on a line indicates that the line is to be done in
that color.)

Color Guide

Number	Color Name	Paternayan Color
1	bright dark orange	#958
2	bright orange	#968
3	orange	#434
4	medium light orange	#444
5	dark kelly green	#559
6	kelly green	#569
7	medium light kelly green	#589
8	dark yellow	#427
9	lemon yellow	#450
10	pale yellow	#458
11	white	#005

Figure III-56. Graph Outline.

Spring Daisies

Footstool-Cover Design (Shown on a Footstool)

For a sunny, yellow and white living room, yellow and white daisies bring the freshness of the outdoors inside.

Figure III-57. Spring Daisies design. Worked and owned by Mrs. Edward G. Bazelon.

Figure III-58. Detailed view of *Spring Daisies* design. The design is 17 inches (43.2 cm) in diameter.

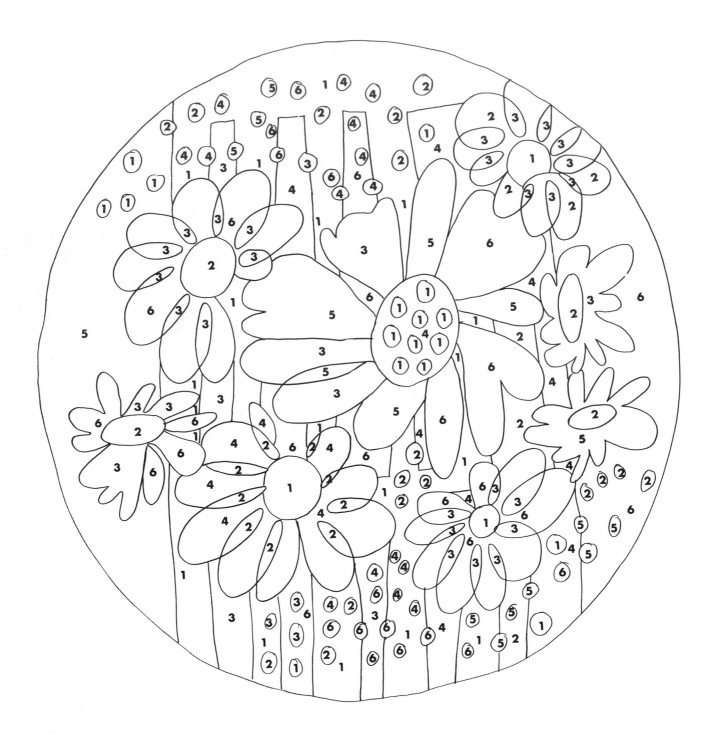

Figure III-59. Color Chart Outline.

Color Guide

Number	Color Name	Paternayan Color
1	dark yellow	#427
2	medium dark yellow	#440
3	yellow	#441
4	medium light yellow	#442
5	light yellow	#438
6	white	#005

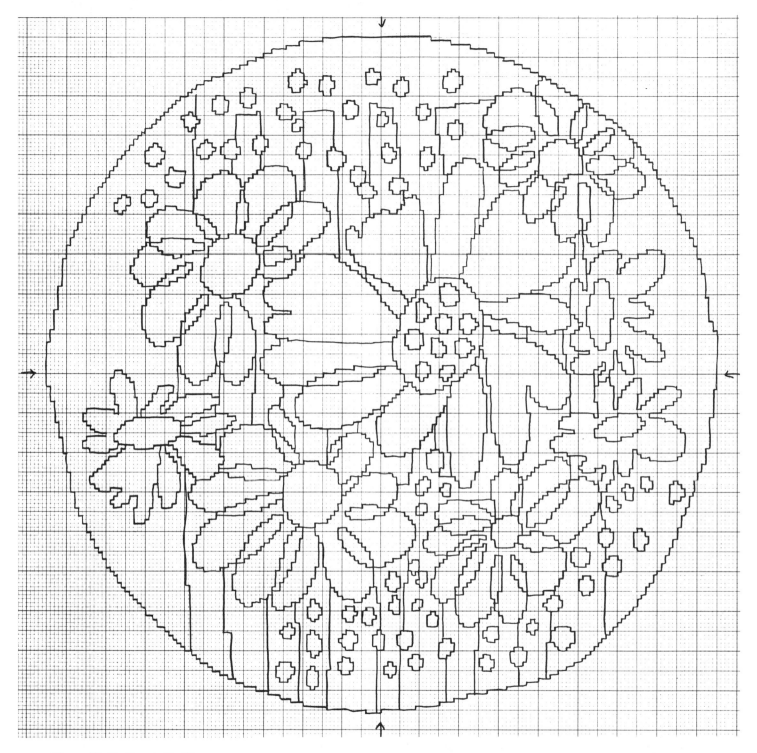

Figure III-60. Graph Outline.

117

Contemporary Circles

Seat Design (Shown on a Contemporary Chair)

Circles in many sizes make a pleasing pattern. The variety of sizes makes the same shape more interesting and changes the dynamics of the design.

Figure III-61. Contemporary Circles design. Worked and owned by Mrs. Edward G. Bazelon.

Figure III-62. Detail of *Contemporary Circles* design. The chair is 20 inches long and 21 inches wide (50.8 cm by 53.3 cm).

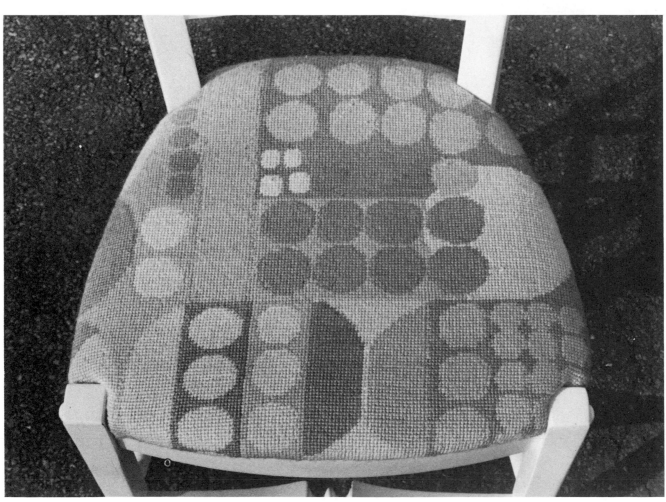

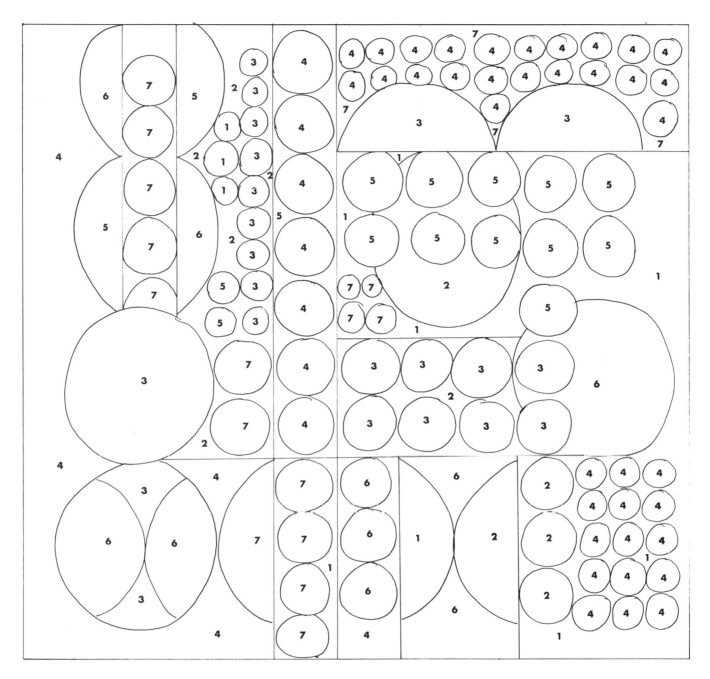

Figure III-63. Color Chart Outline.

Color Guide

Number	Color Name	Paternayan Color
1	deep pink	#855
2	red pink	#860
3	deep peach	#260
4	medium peach	#265
5	yellow	#442
6	light yellow	#437
7	pale yellow	#468

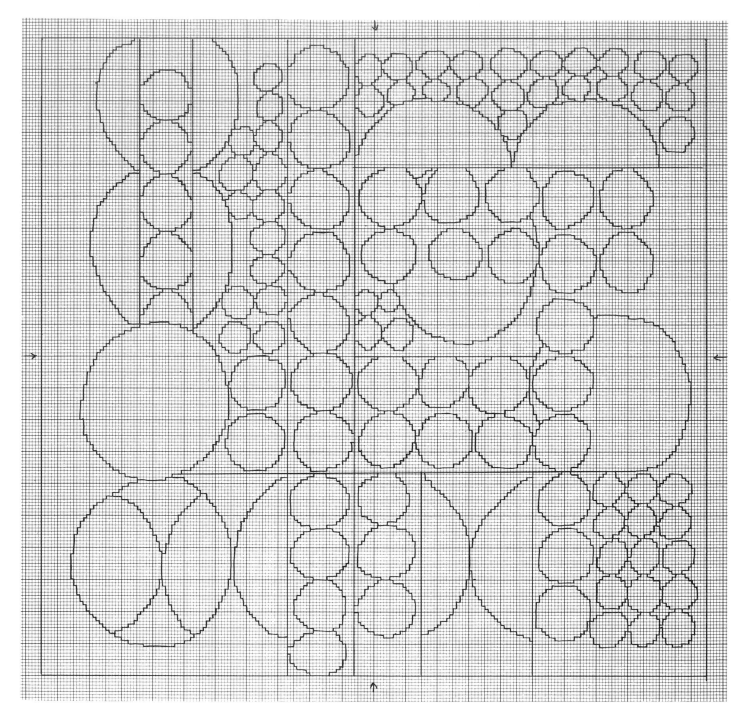

Figure III-64. Graph Outline.

Chair and Plants Collage

Chair-Pad Design (Shown on a Bertoia/Knoll Chair)

The form of the Bertoia chair is a favorite of mine. It is to me as much a piece of sculpture as all the other art Harry Bertoia has created. This popular chair is manufactured by Knoll International. It is a classic chair in the same sense the basic Thonet chair is. It is unquestionably beautiful, universally useful, light and sturdy.

Figure III-65. Chair and Plants Collage design. Worked and owned by Judith Gross.

Figure III-66. Detail of *Chair and Plants Collage* design. The pad is 16½ inches long and 18½ inches wide (41.9 cm by 47 cm). *Note:* The needlepoint seat pad designed by Judith Gross is not a standard feature of the 420 Bertoia Side Chair offered by Knoll International.

To create the chair-pad design I photographed the chair and used parts of my photo prints to work a collage. Also in the collage were other photographs taken of plants in my dining room where the plants and chairs live together. The collage turned out to be the right pattern for the fabric. So I needlepointed it to make pads for the chairs. I was so pleased with the first pad that I had an inspiration for the other five in my set. Using the same design with five shades of the same four colors plus white in each chair, I progressively intermingled the colors and shades. In that way no two pads are alike, yet they all have the same pattern and related coloring. The result is fascinating, but not boisterous or incongruous.

My color charts demonstrate how you can achieve a similar effect and can utilize shades from light to dark and from dark to light. Follow the Color Guide numbers for placement of each yarn color. A is for the Chair Pad shown; B, C, D, E and F, for the others in the six-piece set.

Pad A Color Guide

Number	Color Name	Paternayan Color
1	dark red	#207
2	medium dark red	#240
3	red	#242
4	medium light red	#132
5	light red	#138
6	dark khaki	#124
7	medium dark khaki	#134
8	khaki	#136
9	medium light khaki	#541
10	light khaki	#020
11	white	#005

Pad B Color Guide

Number	Color Name	Paternayan Color
1	dark yellow	#427
2	medium dark yellow	#440
3	yellow	#441
4	medium light yellow	#442
5	light yellow	#438
6	dark khaki	#124
7	medium dark khaki	#134
8	khaki	#136
9	medium light khaki	#541
10	light khaki	#020
11	white	#005

Pad C Color Guide

Number	Color Name	Paternayan Color
1	dark red	#207
2	medium dark red	#240
3	red	#242
4	medium light red	#132
5	light red	#138
6	dark yellow	#427
7	medium dark yellow	#440
8	yellow	#441
9	medium light yellow	#442
10	light yellow	#438
11	white	#005

Pad D Color Guide

Number	Color Name	Paternayan Color
1	dark yellow	#427
2	medium dark yellow	#440
3	yellow	#441
4	medium light yellow	#442
5	light yellow	#438
6	dark red	#207
7	medium dark red	#240
8	red	#242
9	medium light red	#132
10	light red	#138
11	white	#005

Pad E Color Guide

Number	Color Name	Paternayan Color
1	dark green	#540
2	medium green	#553
3	green	#590
4	medium light green	#593
5	light green	#040
6	dark yellow	#427
7	medium dark yellow	#440
8	yellow	#441
9	medium light yellow	#442
10	light yellow	#438
11	white	#005

Pad F Color Guide

Number	Color Name	Paternayan Color
1	dark yellow	#427
2	medium dark yellow	#440
3	yellow	#441
4	medium light yellow	#442
5	light yellow	#438
6	dark green	#540
7	medium dark green	#553
8	green	#590
9	medium light green	#593
10	light green	#040
11	white	#005

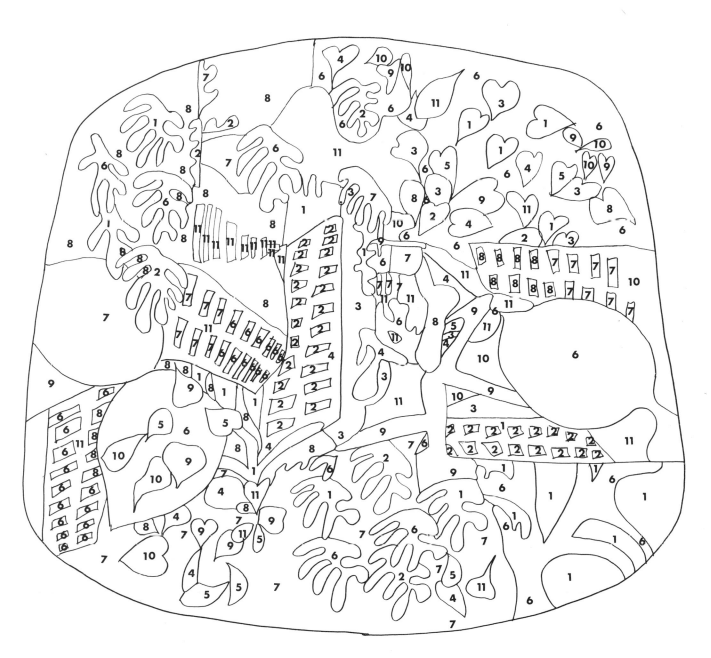

Figure III-67. Color Chart Outline.

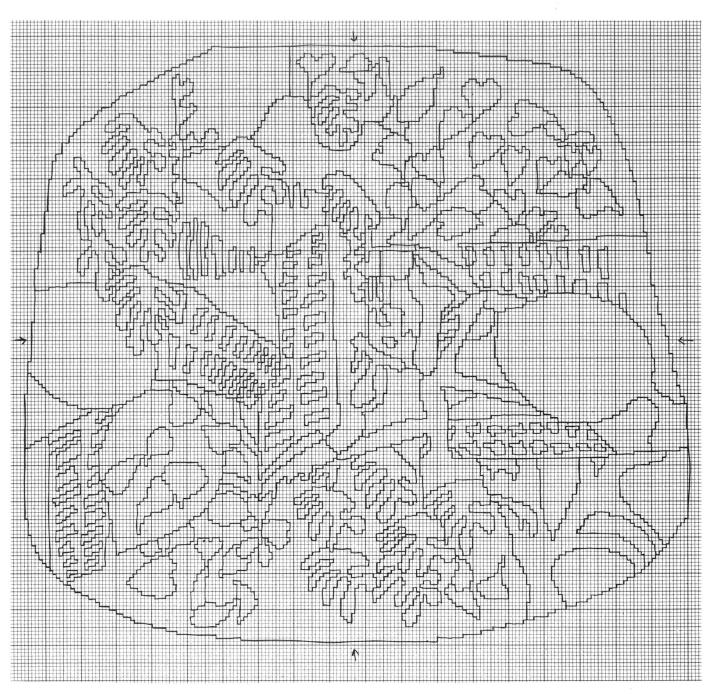

Figure III-68. Graph Outline.

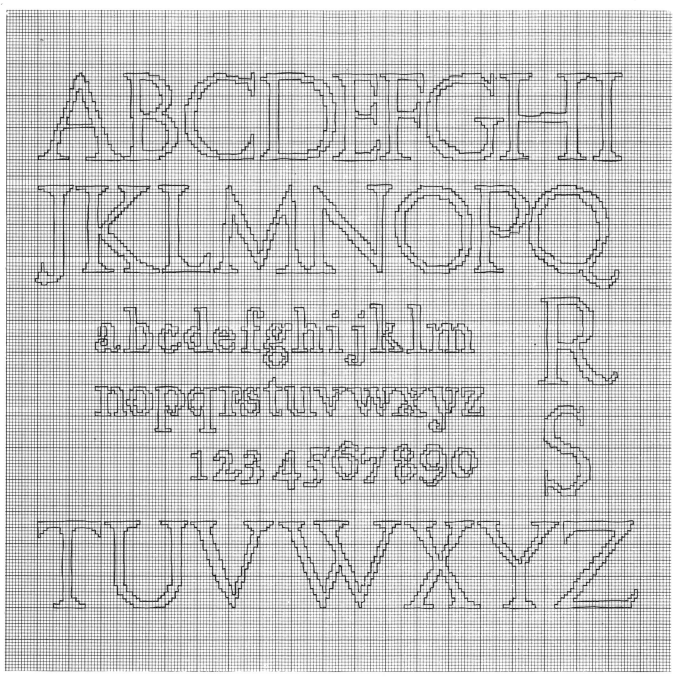

Figure III-69. Alphabet and numbers for needlepointing.

BIBLIOGRAPHY

Books

Albers, Josef. *Interaction of Color*. New Haven, Connecticut: Yale University Press, 1963.

Bishop, Robert. *Centuries and Styles of The American Chair 1640–1970*. New York: E. P. Dutton & Co., Inc., 1972.

Buchwald, Hans H. *Form From Process—The Thonet Chair*. Cambridge, Massachusetts: Carpenter Center for the Visual Arts, Harvard University, Fall and Winter, 1967.

Drepperd, Carl W. *Handbook of Antique Chairs*. Garden City, New York: Doubleday & Company, Inc., 1948.

Dyer, Walter A. and Fraser, Esther Stevens. *The Rocking Chair, an American Institution*. New York and London: The Century Co., 1928.

Hanley, Hope. *Needlepoint*. New York; Charles Scribner's Sons, 1964.

Herzogenrath, Wulf. *50 Years Bauhaus* An International Exhibition. Chicago, Illinois: Illinois Institute of Technology, Crown Hall. August 25 to September 26, 1969.

Johnston, Meda Parker and Kaufman, Glen. *Design on Fabrics*. New York: Reinhold Publishing Corporation, 1967.

Karasz, Mariska. *Adventures in Stitches*. New York: Funk & Wagnalls Publishing Company, Inc., 1949.

Nelson, George. *Chairs*. Interior Library 2. New York: Whitney Publications, Inc., 1953.

Schwartz, Marvin D. *Please Be Seated*. Washington, D.C.: The American Federation of Arts, 1968.

White Chapel Art Gallery London. *Modern Chairs 1918–1970*. Boston, Massachusetts: Boston Book & Art Publisher, 1970.

Periodicals

Craft Horizons
American Craftsmen's Council
44 W. 53rd St.
New York, N.Y. 10019

The Flying Needle
National Standards Council of American Embroiderers
12920 N.E. 32nd Pl.
Bellevue, Wash. 98005

Needle Arts
The Embroiderers' Guild of America, Inc.
6 E. 45th St.
New York, N.Y. 10017

INDEX